GLOBAL GRILLING

GLOBAL GRILLING

SIZZLING RECIPES FROM AROUND THE WORLD

by
Jay Solomon

The Crossing Press
Freedom, CA 95019

Library of Congress Cataloging-in-Publication Data

Solomon, Jay.
    Global grilling : sizzling recipes from around the world / by Jay
Solomon.
        p.   cm.
    Includes index.
    ISBN 0-89594-667-X. -- ISBN 0-89594-666-1 (pbk.)
    1. Barbecue cookery. 2. Cookery, International. I. Title.
TX840.B3S645 1994
641.5'784--dc20   93-45967
                                CIP

Acknowledgments

This cookbook is the synthesis of many years of cooking, writing, traveling and teaching. There have been many people along the way who have contributed to my culinary ventures. I would like to thank Dennis Hayes of the Crossing Press for giving the green light for this cookbook (and earnestly reminding me of impending deadlines). Kathleen Marron at World Variety Produce and Judy Meyenhofer of the Barbecue Industry Association provided valuable products and information. And my cooking classes at The Boston Center for Adult Education and in Ithaca, New York, have given me a forum to test many of my new ideas.

Throughout my career, I have depended upon the valuable advice and feedback of my family, friends, students, customers, and editors. I am lucky to have an enthusiastic group of "taste testers" who have graciously listened to me carry on about the depth of thyme, the nuance of nutmeg, and so forth. Special thanks go to Jessica Robin, Beth Ryan, Claire and Michele Terrelonge, Helena Das, and to my *primo* culinary confidante, Emily Robin. Thanks also to my far-flung and longtime supporters: Janet Welch, Robert Cima, Shaun Buckley, James Paradiso, Tammy Livengood, Adrienne Nims, Linda and Jon Meyerhoff, Freddi Pollack, and Jeff Lischer.

Finally, I would like to thank my parents, Jesse and Ann Solomon, brother Gregory, sister Lisa, and my grandmother, Mary Badia Solomon.

This book is dedicated to
my close friend and confidante, Emily Robin.

Table of Contents

Introduction

Once considered an elementary method of cooking hamburgers and hot dogs, outdoor grilling has evolved into a global style of sophisticated cooking. Grilling is both an art and a sport, an activity where intuition and taste matter more than science, and where flavors of the world are heightened and the senses are invigorated. *Global Grilling* is filled with appealing and sizzling barbecue recipes from around the world and perfect for the great outdoors.

Here is an array of international dishes that enliven the outdoor barbecue with adventurous flavors and enticing aromas. *Global Grilling* includes marinades, spice rubs, pastes, basting sauces, and accompaniments. The dishes are healthful, diverse and exciting: Thai and Indonesian Satays, Jamaican Jerk Barbecue, Asian Teriyaki and Yakitori, Campfire Fajitas, South American Barbecue, Greek Souvlaki, Middle Eastern Shish Kebabs, and All-American Serious Barbecued Ribs are some of the globally inspired meals.

Grilling is both a universal and personal experience. While growing up, when my father came home from work clutching a bag of fresh corn and steaks, I dropped what I was doing. We'd fire up the grill; while it heated, we prepared kebabs and salads with the rest of my family. Visits to relatives or to the park meant an outdoor barbecue was in the works. To this day, whenever I smell the aroma of charcoal fire in the air, warm thoughts of anticipation rush through my mind.

Years later, as restaurant owner and chef, I hovered over the coal's red glare every night, grilling for a dining room full of customers and marveling at how the fire seared, sizzled and dazzled in front of me. Grilling was now my craft.

On my epicurean travels throughout the world, I searched for adventurous fare wherever I ate, always in pursuit of a local barbecue, perhaps a new taste of fire and spice.

A World of Flavors

For centuries, people all over the planet have been cooking over fire. One can only imagine the elation our ancestors felt when fire was tamed for the first barbecue. The method spread to every continent, and a plethora of grilled meals evolved over time, shaped by culture, climate, vegetation and access to land and sea. The grilling legacies are as varied as the cuisines.

Satays are the grilled dishes of Indonesia, Thailand, Malaysia, and other parts of Southeast Asia. It is an ancient method of skewering and marinating everything from shellfish and chicken to beef, pork, and lamb. Satays are often served with a spicy satay peanut sauce. In other parts of Asia, *teriyaki* was the grilling dish: a soy-based marinade with a variety of combinations, including sesame oil, ginger, garlic, pepper, orange or pineapple juice. Another Japanese version, *yakitori,* is a lightly sweet basting sauce.

In Hawaii and other islands of the Pacific, pits were dug into the earth and lined with rocks, forming an *imu.* The fire was made with banana leaves and wood, and pork and fish were seasoned and slowly barbecued. Even today, any special occasion is celebrated with a grilling feast, (a *luau*), typically along the scenic beaches.

On the other side of the world, the Caribbean is a hotbed of grilling culture, most notably in Jamaica, where jerk barbecue is king. Jamaicans slather barbecued meat, chicken and fish with herbs, spices and the fiery Scotch bonnet peppers. Jerk barbecue pits (comes from "to jerk the meat back and forth") line the roads of Jamaica. Other islands, such as Barbados, Trinidad, and Puerto Rico are known for green seasoning pastes, mixtures of herbs and spices served at the table or as a marinade.

In the Mediterranean region, herbal marinades became popular. Greek *souvlakis*, Italian *speidinis* and garlic-scented Portuguese and Spanish seafood light up the Mediterranean grill.

In addition, a tradition of rich sauces and pastes such as pesto, *aioli*, *skordalia*, and *tzatziki* has adorned grilled food. In the nearby Middle East, grilled lamb and beef shish kebabs were stuffed into pita bread with vegetables, and fish were served with tahini sauces.

Tandoori is an Indian method of marinating and roasting chicken or fish in a *tandoor* clay oven. Tandoori is seasoned with yogurt, cumin, coriander, chili peppers, and ginger. The tandoori marinade tenderizes the chicken and imbues a delicate, smoky flavor with a hint of fire. Afghan *tikka* kebabs are similar in flavor to the Indian tandoori barbecue, and omnipresent at town bazaars. Africans serve grilled fare with ground nut sauces, an earthy peanut paste with a penetrating flavor.

Fajitas evolved as a Tex-Mex attempt to tenderize tough, flavorless cuts of beef like skirt steak. The fajitas were marinated and served on a sizzling platter with a mini-buffet of salsa, cheese, sour cream, tortillas, grilled onions and green peppers. The primary flavors are lime, oregano and garlic.

In Mexico, *barbacoa* is the term for barbecue, and is often accompanied by spicy salsas and sauces. Tomatoes, tomatillos, citrus juices, fresh herbs, and a plethora of chilies inspire a different salsa for any occasion. Spice rubs and pastes are also prevalent, especially in the grilled food of the Yucatan.

In many parts of South America, grilling is a way of life. *Churrassco* means barbecue, and every country offers its own version of an outdoor table sauce—*molho* in Brazil, *pebre* in Chile, and *chimichuri* in Argentina. Most of the sauces are tart mixtures of parsley, cilantro, onions and chilies.

Of course, America is known for the down home barbecue, the slow cooking of pork and chicken in a smoky chamber. While hamburger and hot dogs have been linked to American grilling in the past, more than ever the American cook-out has become a hotbed for global grilling, a grand melting pot of all of the world's cuisines cooked over fire. From the heartland's barbecued ribs and chicken to the coastal cuisine of grilled fish and vegetables, America's barbecue scene is constantly heating up.

I have had many years to contemplate and appreciate the wonders, joy and beauty of outdoor grilling. I have collected the culmination of these culinary experiences and travels into this cookbook. With *Global Grilling*, you can splice the flavors of the world's cuisines with the spirit of the great outdoors. So start slicing and dicing, fire up your outdoor grill, and prepare yourself for a taste of the *Global Grilling*, the world's oldest and newest cooking sensation. Happy grilling!

The Art of
Grilling

Outdoor grilling is a universal social experience practiced the world over. It is an event as well as a meal; everything from extravagant celebrations to simple gatherings of family and friends has taken place around the grill. And since it is an ongoing interactive experience—you don't just place the roast in the oven and set the timer—there are a few things to think about ahead of time to ensure a successful and pleasure-filled meal. You want to be surrounded by smiling faces when the food is served.

For purists, here is a clarification of terms: Grilling means cooking food directly over the hot coals. The food is seared and cooks quickly. Barbecuing refers to a slow cooking method at low temperature, usually over indirect heat. The food is cooked with smoke and heat. A steak or fish fillet is grilled; large cuts of meat, fish and poultry are barbecued. With that said, it's safe to say that the terms are interchangeable in most parts of the country.

Mastering the technique of grilling requires practice, vigilance, and wise judgment. It is both an art and a sport, a place where intuition matters more than science, and where, ultimately, an aesthetic sense of taste reigns over any cookbook or how-to manual. It involves split-second decisions as well as preparation and planning. The proper grilling temperature, tools, and a well-seasoned grill also contribute to the grilling equation.

Types of Grills

There are many kinds of grills and everyone seems to have a favorite. I grew up with a simple backyard kettle fueled with charcoal. Some people with large families build elaborate cinderblock or brick ovens. On camping trips, I have had spectacular meals grilled over branches and twigs. At my restaurant, I learned to appreciate the efficiency of gas-fired grills with ceramic coals.

The kind of grill you use depends upon how often you plan to grill, how many people you'll entertain, what food you prefer, and your personal tastes. Here is a brief description of some types of grills, fireboxes and fuels available.

Charcoal Grills

There are a variety of charcoal grills, ranging from rectangular-shaped hibachis or braziers to large round kettles held up with tripod-like legs and covered with a dome-shaped lid. The charcoal sits in a firebox and is ignited; after about 20 minutes, it radiates heat. Some grills have covers, vents, and adjustable grates. The large rectangular grills with lids are called covered cookers or grill wagons.

Gas Grills

If anything has revolutionized the backyard barbecue, it has been the emergence of gas-fired grills. With a turn of the wrist, an outdoor barbecue is a few minutes away, and you don't have to get your hands dirty. The fuel is most often provided by refillable liquid propane tanks. The grate is filled with ceramic briquettes or lava rocks; the rocks absorb the heat and in turn radiate heat which cooks the food. They can be used with or without a lid. The heat is adjustable.

Some barbecuing snobs claim that gas-fired grills lack true grilling flavor. At my restaurant, on busy nights the entire block would smell of the grilled food, and people on the street would come in and ask "What smells so good?" What's my point?

Successful grilling is about cooking over fire with skill, creativity, and a sense of taste. The food is what matters most, including the marinade, spice rub, or condiment used. The source of the heat is only part of the equation. There are wood chips available to add to the cooker for additional smoke.

Water Smoker

This is a tall, cylindrical, silo-looking smokehouse oven. The coals are at the bottom and a water pan sits above the coals, and above the water pan rests the grid for food. If you have a lot of time on your hands, this method is for you. The food slowly cooks in the smoke and steam. Food cooked in this fashion is moist, tender, and reeking of a smokehouse. It is ideal for ribs, briskets, and whole chicken, duck, and turkey. It seems to be a midwestern thing.

Choosing the Fuel

The amount of grilling you do may influence the kind of fuel you should use. Here is a rundown of what's out there.

Charcoal Briquettes

Charcoal is made by burning wood in an oxygen-depleted environment, and the result is a carbon mass. Henry Ford actually pioneered the process of making briquettes when he was looking for a use for the wood by-products from the Model T frames. Some chemicals and binding agents are added, and the mass is shaped into a brick.

Believe it or not, there is a difference in charcoal. There are varying qualities of briquettes, so try different brands until you find one that you like. Some take forever to generate heat, and others give off a gas-like odor. Charcoal briquettes should give off a smoky barbecue flavor.

Instant Lighting Briquettes

Touch a match and "poof!", the coals are on fire. No starter fluid or paper is necessary. Some brands don't even have to be opened; just set the bag in the firebox and set ablaze. It's convenient but expensive.

Lump Charcoal

Lump charcoal comes in inconsistent sizes or shapes and must be broken up before using. It does create a more intense fire than briquettes so less is needed. Lump charcoal contains no additives, starts quicker, and provides a clean, long-lasting fire. However, it does occasionally throw sparks. Some chefs swear by lump charcoal.

Hardwood

The world's original fuel, wood, is now considered something of a specialty item. There are a variety of woods and wood chips available. One of the better known woods, mesquite, is a renegade tree grown throughout the Southwest traced as far back as to the Aztecs. Mesquite burns for a long time and imparts an intense aroma to steaks, pork, wild game and strongly flavored fish. Mesquite-fired ovens and grills have appeared all over America, and this gnarly, scrubby tree has become a hot commodity.

Hickory is the favorite wood for barbecued ribs and meat roasts. Fruity woods, such as apple, cherry, and mango tree are favored for poultry and fish. Other woods, including maple and oak, have their own following. In Hawaii, *kiawe* is a popular version of mesquite.

Wood Chips and Other Added Products

Here is a way to incorporate the flavor of wood with the convenience of charcoal or gas grills. Adding wood chips to the fire (or in a pan) instills a smoky flavor to the grill.

The chips have to be soaked in water before they are added. The resulting smoke is close to the real thing. Mesquite, hickory, and maple wood chips fare well.

Some cooks like to add vines, herbs, and tree cuttings to the fire. Here's my philosophy about herbs: If you desire an herbal flavor, use the herbs in a marinade, spice rub or paste; adding vines produces smoke, but not any recognizable flavor.

Starting the Fire

Years ago, I wrote a monthly food column for a weekly newspaper. A "friend" of mine once delightfully told me that he had discovered the best use of all for one of my food stories. He used it to start his charcoal fire.

Even if you don't have one of my old food columns, there are several other ways to ignite a charcoal fire. The most common is with lighter fluid: Squirt the fluid on the briquettes and let it soak in for a few minutes. Touch a match and allow the coals to burn for 15 to 20 minutes, allowing the petroleum odor to burn off. Never, never add additional lighter fluid to charcoal that has already been lit. (Presoaked briquettes, of course, do not need lighter fluid).

Building a fire with kindling, such as dry branches, wood trimmings, etc, is another way to ignite a fire. The coals are added as the fire grows in intensity. This is a high maintenance method and requires lots of patience to nurture and feed the fire.

The electrical starter, usually in the shape of a loop, is an easy way to start a fire if you have access to an electrical outlet and a durable extension cord. The loop is set in the coals and removed when they ignite. Some people appreciate the consistent and clean nature of this method. One thing: Have an idea in mind where to set the hot loop when you remove it. A fireproof surface is a good place. Not near a place where someone is going to sit down.

Using a metal chimney, or flue, is another clean and efficient method. It is a cylindrical, coffee can-shaped container, with charcoal sitting on a top grate and crumpled-up newspaper stuffed in the bottom section. The paper is set on fire and the draft sends heat pulsing through the coals. When the coals are ashen colored, spread them around a grill.

Controlling the heat is a prime concern. Most covered grills have vents in the firebox and cover. When the grill is covered and the vents are open, the air flow allows the fuel to burn hotter. When closed, the decreased level of air flow reduces the heat of the fuel. Uncovered, the coals burn the hottest. Gas grills of course have temperature settings.

So it is important to start with the proper heat level. If a grill temperature is too low, the product will remain on the grill longer and consequently dry out. If the grill heat is too high, the outside will char and leave the inside raw. The cook must know where the hot and warm spots are on the grill.

The challenge is to "sear and seal": sear the product while sealing in the juices. Grid marks impress a great deal. Charred corners do not, and should be avoided or trimmed.

For an open grill, here is an easy way to test the heat:

Hold the palm of your hand over the grill near the grate. If you can keep your hand there for less than two seconds, it is too hot. If you hold it for 3 to 4 seconds, it is the optimal grilling temperature for steaks, kebabs, fillets and shellfish. Hold it for 5 seconds, and it is the best level for whole fish, barbecued whole poultry, large cuts of meats, and vegetables.

The best time to clean the grill is just after you've removed the food. A steel wire brush is the best tool for cleaning the grill. The firebox and coals or bricks should also be cleaned on a regular basis. When ashes accumulate, the air flow and efficiency decrease and the cooking time increases.

Preparing Your Grilling Station

In college, I trained at a student-run restaurant. At the beginning of every shift this guy would walk around the kitchen screaming "*mise-en-place, mise-en-place, mise-en-place,*" like a broken record. What a jerk. He was trying to encourage us to get our stations set up, get our utensils in place, and get our house in order. Even if you were prepared, he'd yell it at you.

The message was important, even if the messenger was an idiot. There is nothing worse than scrambling for a plate or utensil during a crucial moment at the grilling position. Take a few minutes to organize your grilling station. Assemble all of your ingredients on a table near the grill within arm's reach.

Grilling Accoutrements

Every grill chef has a trusty inventory of tools and utensils. I favor using hard plastic tongs to turn food whenever possible. Many cultures rely on skewers or sticks to hold food while it grills. My grandmother gave me a set of metal skewers with elaborate wooden handles that had been handed down through three generations.

The following is an inventory that a master grill chef might own.

Tongs. At my restaurant, tongs were like another appendage to me, an extension of my hand. Tongs are absolutely essential for successful grilling. With tongs, you can turn, move, reposition and remove almost any item on the grill. The tongs should be durable with wide claws and opened and closed with a spring loaded resistance and assistance.

Spatula. A long-handled, rectangular-shaped spatula is essential for flipping burgers, large steaks, fish fillets and whole fish. I use it in conjunction with tongs.

Long-handled Fork. In the old days, grill chefs stuck a fork into almost everything on the grill to peek for doneness, and the juices spilled out and the food looked like a machine gun had riddled it. Over time cooks discovered the utility of spatulas and tongs, and the sight of a chef holding a fork is a bit anachronistic. Forks are essentially a tool to stir the coals or move the grate. They will hold a large piece of meat to slice for doneness.

Skewers. I prefer long metal skewers that have a handle of some sort at one end. There are also disposable bamboo and wood skewers which have a tendency to singe at the ends. Metal skewers are durable and enable you to turn cubed meat, chicken, fish and shellfish with ease.

Grill Brush. Alas, there comes a time when the grill surface must be scrubbed. I use a long-handled wire brush with sharp strands. The grill should be cleaned after you remove the food. This requires discipline, but it is the mark of a real grill chef if you leave the grill clean. There's nothing worse than placing a beautiful swordfish steak on a grill laden with gristle.

You may also need the following:

- Fish basket
- Large knife
- Large metal or foil pan (to place the grilled food in)
- Aluminum foil
- Large bowl (to rest the skewers on)
- Cutting board

- Towels, napkins, plateware, silverware, and glasses
- Hot sauce, salt and pepper shaker or pepper mill and fresh lemons and limes;
- All of the ingredients you intend to grill
- Plenty of beverages to pass around
- A backup fuel source (for gas-fired grills with liquid propane tanks that eventually run out)
- Fire extinguisher or water spray bottle (you never know when you'll need it)

Aside from imparting a outdoorsy smokiness to food, grilling enables the cook to dramatically influence the flavor and texture in a variety of ways. Marinades impart flavor while tenderizing grilled foods. Spice rubs and pastes are a quick and easy way to flavor grilled items at the last minute and produce a coat of flavor. Accompaniments include sauces and condiments, such as salsas, chutneys, and barbecue sauces, and are served with the grilled food at the table. This book is about the many authentic and innovative ways to rejuvenate grilled foods.

Appetizers, Salads and Sandwiches

This chapter offers grilled entrées intended for light meals or appetizers. The selection of grilled appetizers, salads and sandwiches departs from the normal fare, but with good reason. There is a whole new world order of eclectic small dishes that bring flair and flavor to the grill.

These dishes encompass a wide range of blazing good ways to start a meal: Swordfish Souvlaki with Mesclun and Feta Salad, Rum Soaked Calypso Beef Salad, and Scorched Conch and Rocotillo Salad are a few of the selections. Quick and colorful fare such as Grilled Antipasto with Basil Oil and Gado-Gado with Foil Wrapped Vegetables display grilled vegetables in an entirely different (and appealing) light.

For years, the Chicken Teriyaki and Avocado Sandwich reigned supreme at my restaurant, easily more popular than hamburgers. Yet, when hamburgers did appear on the grill, it was with much fanfare and panache. Blue Cheese Burger with Beet Horseradish Catsup and the Ragin' Cajun Burger offer a new perspective on the traditional fare.

From the simple but satisfying Grilled Bread and Oil and Roasted Squash with Nutmeg and Rosemary to the enticing Campfire Chicken Fajita Salad and Bob's Down Home Clambake, this chapter embraces spirited dishes for light dining on their own or as a prelude to an exciting dinner to come.

Grilled Bread and Oil

SICILY/GREECE

My mother has fond memories of her visits to Sicily, her parents' homeland. One of her favorite dishes was the simplest: Grilled bread dipped in oil. Bread and oil is also served in northern Italy and Greece as a precursor to the meal to come.

1 loaf Italian bread (unsliced)
1/4 cup olive oil
4 garlic cloves, slivered
Fresh ground black pepper, to taste

Preheat the grill until the coals are gray to white.

Place the oil and garlic in a serving bowl.

When the fire is ready, place the bread on the grill. Heat the bread until a crust begins to form, about 5 to 7 minutes.

Transfer the bread to a cutting board and cut into thick slices. Dip the bread into the oil and sprinkle with the pepper.

Yield: 4 to 6 servings

Grilled Chicken, Ce-Ci Bean and Bow Tie Salad

ITALY

Hot grilled chicken combines with chilled pasta to produce a dynamic salad. Bow ties (farfalle) pasta have an eponymous shape and make for a eye catching presentation. Ce-ci (pronounced *chee-chee*), which are more commonly known as chickpeas or garbanzo beans, have a nutty taste and chewy texture. Add fresh basil and a balsamic vinaigrette and you have a very pretty culinary picture.

8 ounces bow tie pasta (farfalle)
8 to 10 cherry tomatoes, halved
4 scallions, chopped
1 yellow or green pepper, seeded and diced
1 1/2 cups ce-ci beans (chick-peas)
1/2 cup olive oil
1/4 cup balsamic vinegar or red wine vinegar
1/4 cup fresh basil leaves, chopped
6 to 8 pepperoncini, chopped
2 garlic cloves, minced
2 tablespoons minced fresh parsley
1/2 teaspoon salt
1/4 teaspoon red pepper flakes
1/4 cup grated Parmesan cheese
1/2 pound boneless, skinless chicken breasts, pounded out

Place the bow ties in boiling water to cover and cook for 12 minutes, until al dente (tender). Drain in colander and cool under cold running water. Chill for 15 minutes.

In a large bowl, combine the tomatoes, scallions, pepper, ce-ci beans, oil, vinegar, basil, pepperoncini, garlic and seasonings. Add the pasta and cheese and toss together thoroughly. Chill for 30 minutes to 1 hour.

Preheat the grill until the coals are gray to white.

When the fire is ready, place the chicken on the oiled grill. Cook for 5 to 7 minutes on each side, until white in the center. Remove the chicken and toss with the pasta salad. Serve at once or chill.

Yield: 4 servings

Scorched Conch
and Rocotillo Salad

BAHAMAS

Visitors to the Bahamas soon discover the favorite Bahamian food: Conch. The shellfish meat is in everything—soups, stews, fritters, salads, you name it. My favorite is conch salad. For the best conch salad, head to the bridge that connects Paradise Island, where islanders extract the conch from the shell and assemble the salad right in front of you. The shells are for sale, too.

Although conch is not readily available on the mainland, it does sporadically appear at the fish market. Shrimp or scallops may also be used for this salad. Authentic conch salad is prepared without cooking, in the style of seviche—it "cooks" in the lime juice. But when I am in landlocked Ithaca, far from the islands, I prefer to grill the conch first. Conch has a rubbery texture, but pounding it with a mallet before grilling will tenderize it somewhat.

The rocotillo pepper, (also called *ajisito*) provides a pleasant kick. It is shaped like miniature patty pan squash and has the floral flavor (but much less heat) of a Scotch bonnet pepper.

1 tomato, cored and finely chopped
1/4 cup minced red onion
1/2 Scotch bonnet pepper or 2 to 3 rocotillo
  peppers, seeded and minced
Juice of 1 lime or lemon
1/2 teaspoon salt
1 pound fresh conch meat, pounded out

Combine all of the ingredients, except the conch, in a large bowl. Set aside.

Preheat the grill until the coals are gray to white.

When the fire is ready, place the conch on the grill. Cook for 5 to 7 minutes, until opaque in the center. Occasionally turn while it cooks.

Remove the conch from the grill, chop, and add to the tomato mixture. Serve warm or chill for 1 hour.

Yield: 4 servings

Salata Mechouia

TUNISIA

Roasted or grilled salads are a prevalent fixture in Tunisian kitchens. The vegetable *salata* (or salad) makes a flavorful side dish to grilled fish or chicken.

2 green or red bell peppers
2 large tomatoes
1 red onion, peeled and quartered
3 to 4 garlic cloves, minced
1/4 cup olive oil
2 tablespoons lemon juice
1/2 teaspoon ground cumin
1/4 teaspoon salt
1/4 teaspoon cayenne pepper

Preheat the grill until the coals are gray to white.

When the fire is ready, place the vegetables on the grill. Cook for 5 to 7 minutes, until tender. Occasionally turn the vegetables while they cook.

Remove the vegetables from the grill and coarsely chop. Remove the seeds from the peppers. Add the vegetables to a bowl and combine with the remaining ingredients. Let stand for 30 minutes. Serve with French bread and grilled chicken or fish.

Yield: 4 servings

Wilted Leek, Tomato and Feta Salad

MEDITERRANEAN

Leeks have a toned-down onion flavor that is magnified on the grill. For a light summer salad, toss the grilled leeks with garden tomatoes, feta and a light vinaigrette. Leeks do require a thorough rinsing before grilling: Soak the leeks in water for a few minutes and then agitate the water to release the sand trapped between the green stems.

2 large leeks, halved lengthwise
2 large tomatoes, halved widthwise
2 tablespoons olive or vegetable oil
1 tablespoon balsamic vinegar or
  red wine vinegar
2 tablespoons chopped fresh basil or
  1 teaspoon dried
1/2 cup crumbled feta cheese
Salt and pepper, to taste

Place the leeks in a large bowl and fill with cold water. Remove as much sand as possible from the leaves. Drain and dry the leeks.

Preheat the grill until the coals are gray to white.

Place the leeks and tomatoes on the oiled grill. Cook for 5 to 7 minutes on each side, until the leeks are hatch-marked and tender and the tomatoes are juicy. Transfer the vegetables to a cutting board and coarsely chop. Place in a mixing bowl.

Add the oil, vinegar, basil, and feta to the bowl and toss thoroughly. Season with salt and pepper to taste and serve warm.

Yield: 4 servings

Roasted Squash with Nutmeg and Rosemary

ST. LUCIA

This recipe was inspired by an appetizer I tasted in St. Lucia, an island in the Caribbean. Breadfruit, a soccer ball-shaped starchy fruit, was roasted on the grill and seasoned with herbs and butter. While breadfruit is difficult to find up north, I applied the idea to winter squash, and achieved splendid results. Roasted acorn and delicata squash both have mellow, sweet potato-like flavors, and are loaded with beta carotene.

2 winter squash, halved
4 to 6 fresh rosemary or thyme branches
2 tablespoons butter
About 1/2 teaspoon ground nutmeg

Preheat the grill until the coals are gray to white.

With a sharp-edged spoon, remove the seeds from the center of each squash. Place a rosemary branch and about 1/2 tablespoon of butter in each shell and sprinkle with nutmeg. Wrap the squash in aluminum foil and place on the grill. Cook for 30 to 45 minutes over low heat, occasionally turning the squash.

When the squash is easily pierced with fork, remove it from the grill. Unwrap the squash and serve as a side dish with any grilled dish.

Yield: 4 servings

Ragin' Cajun Burger

CAJUN/USA

Early in my career, long before I became a chef, I was a burger flipper for a major fast food chain . . . . Do I hear someone snickering? Does someone have a problem with that? I won a Silver Spatula award, so *now* who's laughing?

Okay, okay, actually I'd rather forget about that period of my life. However, later on at my first restaurant, the Ragin' Cajun burger became a big lunch item, and my burger experience paid off. The spicy blend of seasonings leaves a well-rounded zing at the tip of the tongue.

1 1/2 pounds lean ground chuck
1 green pepper, seeded and minced
1 medium size onion, minced
1 jalapeño pepper, seeded and minced
1 tablespoon red hot sauce
2 teaspoons dried oregano
1/2 teaspoon ground thyme
1/2 teaspoon red pepper flakes
1/2 teaspoon ground black pepper
1/2 teaspoon cayenne pepper
4 warmed hamburger buns
1 large tomato, sliced
4 to 5 leaves leaf or romaine lettuce,
  washed and torn
About 1 cup catsup or salsa

Combine the beef, green pepper, onion, and jalapeño peppers in a large bowl. Mix in the red hot sauce and seasonings and shape the meat into 4 burger patties. Chill until ready to grill.

Preheat the grill until the coals are gray to white.

When the fire is ready, place the burgers on the oiled grill and cook to desired degree of doneness (about 3 minutes on each side for rare, 6 minutes for medium, and 8 to 9 minutes for well done). Add cheese (if you wish) before serving the burgers on the buns. Top each with tomato and lettuce, and catsup or salsa.

Serve hot.

Yield: 4 servings

Blue Cheese Burger with Beet Horseradish Catsup

USA

If you are going to grill hamburgers, why not make it a gourmet feast? Plain burgers are boring. Try stuffing your hamburgers with a strongly flavored blue cheese, roquefort or Gorgonzola. Embellish it with a funky condiment like beet horseradish catsup and crisp onions and tomatoes. Your taste buds will sit up and take notice.

For the catsup:

2 cups diced beets
1 small onion, diced
1 large tomato, cored and chopped
1 1/4 cups red wine vinegar
1/2 cup water or apple juice
1/3 cup brown sugar
1 teaspoon chili powder
2 to 3 teaspoons hot sauce
1/2 teaspoon black pepper
1/2 teaspoon salt
1 to 2 tablespoons prepared horseradish

For the burger:

1 1/2 pounds lean ground chuck
1/2 pound crumbled blue cheese, roquefort or Gorgonzola cheese
4 hamburger buns, warmed
1 red onion, slivered
1 large tomato, cored and sliced
4 to 5 leaves leaf or romaine lettuce, torn

To make the catsup, combine the first 10 ingredients in a saucepan and bring to a simmer over medium heat. Cook for 35 to 40 minutes, stirring occasionally. Remove from the heat and stir in the horseradish. Add the mixture to a food processor fitted with a steel blade (or blender) and process for 30 seconds. Set aside or chill.

Preheat the grill until the coals are gray to white.

When the fire is almost ready, divide the ground chuck into 4 round flat patties. Spoon 2 to 3 tablespoons of cheese into the center of each patty and reform into a burger, enveloping the crumbled cheese.

Place the stuffed burgers on the oiled grill and cook to desired doneness (about 3 minutes on each side for rare, 6 minutes for medium, and 8 to 9 minutes for well done).

Serve the burgers on warm buns and spoon the catsup over the burger. Top with the red onion, tomato, and lettuce. Pass the extra catsup at the table and chow down!

Yield: 4 servings

Chicken Teriyaki
and Avocado Sandwich

ASIA

Teriyaki is a simple, yet flavorful soy-based marinade. Although traditionally served as a skewered dish, I've incorporated the flavors into a chicken sandwich. For years I served this version at my restaurant: The full chicken breast is halved, marinated, grilled and then served on a sandwich roll (hamburg style). The chicken can also be served as a full meal with jasmine rice. For the best marinade, use a soy sauce that has no added MSG or sugar, and don't marinate longer than the recommended 4 hours.

A luscious ripe avocado completes the sandwich. You can tell an avocado is ripe by gently pressing your palm against the skin. It should give slightly. The avocado should also be dark green to almost black in color.

For the marinade:
1/2 cup soy sauce
1/2 cup Worcestershire sauce
1/2 cup orange juice
1/4 cup vegetable oil
2 tablespoons minced fresh ginger root
3 to 4 garlic cloves, minced
1 tablespoon sugar
1 teaspoon black pepper
2 (8-ounce) boneless, skinless chicken breasts, pounded out and halved
4 hamburger buns, warmed
1 ripe avocado, peeled, pitted, and sliced
1 large tomato, cored and sliced
4 to 5 leaves leaf or romaine lettuce, torn

Combine all of the marinade ingredients, except the chicken, in large mixing bowl and whisk well. Place the chicken in the marinade and chill for 2 to 4 hours. Stir the marinade after 1 hour.

Preheat the grill until the coals are gray to white.

When the fire is ready, remove the chicken from the marinade and place on the oiled grill. Cook for 5 to 7 minutes on each side, until the chicken is white in the center.

Remove the chicken from the grill and serve on warm buns topped with the avocado, tomato, and lettuce.

Yield: 4 servings

Rum Soaked Calypso Beef Salad

VIRGIN ISLANDS

When I first became a chef, I thought it was time to update the eponymous chef's salad. I wanted to offer a salad which was healthier and more creative than the usual pile of soggy lettuce and anemic fixings. So I adapted this recipe from a meal I had savored in the Virgin Islands, and it quickly became a best seller. The grilled beef, combined with leafy greens and crisp vegetables, is an appealing light dinner or lunch.

1/2 cup rum
1/2 cup soy sauce
1/4 cup vegetable oil
1/4 cup Worcestershire sauce
1/4 cup pineapple juice
4 garlic cloves, minced
1 Scotch bonnet or other chili pepper, seeded and minced
1 tablespoon minced fresh ginger
1 teaspoon ground nutmeg
1 teaspoon ground black pepper
1 1/2 to 2 pounds boneless sirloin or top round steaks, well trimmed and cubed
4 large salads with shredded carrots, slivered red onion, sliced tomatoes, sprouts, and green leaf lettuce

Combine all of the marinade ingredients (except the beef) in a large bowl and whisk well. Add the beef and chill for 2 to 4 hours.

Preheat the grill until the coals are gray to white.

Meanwhile, arrange the salads on serving plates. When the fire is ready, remove the beef from the marinade and place on the oiled grill. (You may also thread it on skewers). Cook for 4 to 5 minutes on each side, until the beef reaches the desired degree of doneness. Remove the beef from the grill and place on the salads. Serve with a vinaigrette dressing and warm bread.

Yield: 4 servings

Grilled Antipasto with Basil Oil

—■—

ITALY

This dish was inspired by a superb meal I had at Cornell's Villa Banfi dining room in the Statler Hotel. It is a simple but flavorful way to grill vegetables. The executive chef, Brian Halloran, was kind enough to describe the ingredients to me during the course of the meal. I scribbled down the recipe over dessert.

1/4 cup fresh basil leaves
1/4 cup olive oil
2 to 3 garlic cloves, minced
4 plum tomatoes, cored and halved
1 large onion, peeled and halved
2 bell peppers, seeded and halved
1 medium unpeeled eggplant, cut widthwise into thin ovals
1 zucchini, cut widthwise into thin ovals
1/2 pound sharp provolone cheese, cut into large cubes
Salt and pepper, to taste

Combine the basil, oil and garlic in a food processor fitted with a steel blade and process for 15 seconds, until smooth. Transfer to a bowl.

Place the vegetables and cheese in a large shallow dish. With a pastry brush, "paint" the vegetables and cheese with the basil-oil mixture. Coat everything completely.

Preheat the grill until the coals are gray to white.

When the fire is ready, place the vegetables on the oiled grill. Cook for 7 to 10 minutes, turning after about 5 minutes. When the tomatoes are ready to burst, pull them off and place them in a salad bowl. Remove the remaining vegetables when they become tender and develop hatch marks and place them in the bowl. When all of the vegetables are done, place the provolone on the grill. Give the grill your full attention. Turn the cheese after about 30 seconds. When the cheese is on the verge of melting, remove it and toss it with the vegetables. Add salt and pepper to taste and serve warm.

Yield: 4 servings

Grilled Shrimp with Wasabi Cocktail Sauce

JAPAN/USA

Wasabi jazzes up traditional cocktail sauce with a sharp, clean jolt. The sauce also goes well with raw clams and oysters.

1 1/2 to 2 tablespoons wasabi powder
1 1/2 to 2 tablespoons water
1/2 cup chili sauce
1/2 cup catsup
1 tablespoon lemon juice
1/2 teaspoon ground black pepper
1/4 teaspoon salt
3 to 4 teaspoons bottled hot sauce
2 pounds large shrimp, peeled and deveined
4 to 5 leaves Romaine lettuce

In a small bowl, combine the wasabi powder and an equal amount of water, forming a paste. Let stand for 5 minutes.

Combine the wasabi paste, chili sauce, catsup, lemon juice, and seasonings in a serving bowl. Set aside.

Preheat the grill until the coals are gray to white.

Thread the shrimp onto skewers. When the fire is ready, place the skewers on the oiled grill. Cook for 5 to 7 minutes on each side, or until the shrimp is pink and firm. Transfer the shrimp to plates lined with a bed of lettuce. Dip the shrimp into the wasabi cocktail sauce.

Yield: 4 servings

Puu Puu Chicken with Maui Onions

POLYNESIA/HAWAII

Puu puu originated as a Polynesian equivalent of hors d'oeuvre, and has since evolved to include the flavors of Asia, Hawaii, and Japan. The irresistible flavor of sweet Maui onions complements the platter. Shrimp, pork, or scallops can also be used with the marinade.

1/3 cup soy sauce
1/4 cup Worcestershire sauce
1/4 cup vegetable oil
1/4 cup mirin (sweet Japanese cooking wine)
1/4 cup pineapple juice
1 tablespoon minced fresh ginger
3 to 4 garlic cloves, minced
1 tablespoon sugar
1 teaspoon ground black pepper
1 1/2 pounds boneless, skinless chicken thighs
2 Maui onions, peeled and quartered

Combine all of the ingredients (except the chicken and onion) in a mixing bowl and whisk well. Place the chicken thighs in the marinade and chill for 2 to 4 hours. After 1 hour, stir the marinade.

Preheat the grill until the coals are gray to white.

Remove the chicken from the marinade and thread onto skewers, alternating with the onion. Place on the oiled grill and cook for 5 to 7 minutes on each side, until the chicken is cooked in the center. Transfer to serving plates and serve hot.

Yield: 4 servings

Bob's Down Home Clambake

NEW ENGLAND

In the seventh grade, my buddy Bob Cima held a clambake and invited the whole school. It was an exciting affair filled with food, games and much mirth. Spin the bottle, bobbing for apples, that sort of thing. I don't know for sure, as I wasn't invited. I wasn't cool enough, apparently. The whole school is there and I'm home playing solitaire. Nice.

I'm not one to hold a grudge, and Bob and I eventually became best friends. (I also helped him pass Spanish class.) Although now a high-powered executive in Europe, Bob still throws a clambake about the same time every year when he comes back to the States. He has the perfect recipe for a clambake: Good company, plenty of clams, and cheap beer.

1/2 pound butter, melted
4 garlic cloves, minced
1/2 cup fresh basil leaves, chopped
Water
1/2 cup dry white wine
1/2 cup lemon juice
4 to 6 dozen cherrystone or Little Neck clams
Cheap beer, on ice

In a saucepan, melt the butter and garlic. Add the basil, remove from the heat, and keep warm.

Preheat the grill until the coals are gray to white.

Fill a large stockpot with about 2 inches of water, wine, and lemon juice. Place the pot on the grill, cover, and bring to a boil. When the water is rolling, gently drop the clams into the bath. Don't stack the clams. Cover and cook for 5 to 10 minutes. When the shells open wide, pull them out with tongs or a slotted spoon and place in a bowl.

Repeat the process with the remaining clams. (For culinary effect, place a few clams directly on the grill around the pot as it cooks. Pass them out as they open up.)

Pass the clams around to the guests. Remove the clam meat with forks and dunk into the basil-butter. Serve with beer and napkins.

Yield: 4 to 6 servings

Campfire Chicken Fajita Salad

AMERICAN SOUTHWEST

I made this Tex-Mex classic while camping in the Rocky Mountains near Colorado Springs. There is something intrinsically rewarding about camping out on the side of a mountain, waking up with the sun, hunting for kindling wood, starting a campfire, drinking in the aroma of the great outdoors, and preparing a feast worthy of the grand surroundings.

For the marinade:
3/4 cup vegetable oil
1/2 cup Worcestershire sauce
1/3 cup lime juice
2 tablespoons red wine vinegar
6 to 8 garlic cloves, minced
1 1/2 tablespoons dried oregano
1 tablespoon brown sugar
1 teaspoon black pepper
1/2 teaspoon salt

For the fajitas:
1 1/2 pounds boneless, skinless chicken breasts, cut into 2-inch-wide strips
1 head leaf lettuce, washed and torn
2 tomatoes, cored and chopped
2 cups shredded Monterey jack or provolone cheese
2 cups of your favorite tomato salsa
2 medium onions, cut into wide slivers
2 green peppers, seeded and cut into wide strips
4 to 6 (6-inch) flour tortillas

Combine all of the marinade ingredients in a bowl and whisk well. Place the chicken in the marinade and chill for 2 to 4 hours, stirring at least once.

Preheat the grill until the coals are gray to white. Meanwhile, place the lettuce, tomatoes, cheese and salsa into serving bowls.

When the fire is ready, remove the chicken from the marinade and place on the grill. Place the onions and peppers around the grill's edge. Cook the chicken for 5 to 7 minutes on each side, until white in the center. Grill the vegetables until tender. Transfer the chicken and vegetables to a large serving plate.

Crisp the flour tortillas by placing them on the grill and flipping after a few seconds. To eat, fill the flour tortillas with the grilled items, tomatoes, lettuce, cheese, and salsa.

Yield: 4 servings

Gado-Gado with Foil Wrapped Vegetables

—■—

INDONESIA

Gado-gado is a popular cooked vegetable salad served with a spicy peanut sauce. Traditionally, gado gado vegetables are steamed or blanched, but grilling in foil packets is an appealing variation. You can make the sauce ahead of time and reheat it over the fire.

For the peanut sauce:

1 tablespoon vegetable oil
1 small onion, diced
2 garlic cloves, minced
1 chili pepper, seeded and minced
1 tablespoon minced fresh ginger
1 cup crunchy peanut butter
1/2 cup water
1/4 cup soy sauce or ketjap manis
1 tablespoon lime juice

For the vegetables:

1 small zucchini, chopped
8 mushrooms, halved
8 broccoli florets
1 1/2 cups chopped leafy greens (spinach, collard greens, or Swiss chard)
1 small unpeeled cucumber, chopped
1 cup bean sprouts

To make the sauce, heat the oil in a saucepan and add the onion, garlic, chili and ginger. Sauté for 5 to 7 minutes. Blend in the peanut butter, water, soy sauce, and lime juice. Cook over low heat for 2 to 3 minutes, stirring frequently. Transfer to a serving bowl and keep warm. If the sauce begins to separate, stir it.

Preheat the grill until the coals are gray to white.

Meanwhile, form the vegetable packets. Lay out 4 (12-inch) squares of aluminum foil. Equally distribute the vegetables onto the squares, and wrap like a present, sealing both ends and folding the sides to meet each other. (Leave a tiny opening for steam to escape).

When the fire is ready, place the packets on the grill. Cook 10 to 12 minutes, until the vegetables are soft. Take the packets off the grill and place on plates. Open the packets and spoon the peanut sauce over the vegetables. Pass the extra sauce at the table.

Yield: 4 servings

Grilled Squid with Fresh Greens

PORTUGAL AND SPAIN

Squid is extremely popular in European countries, especially Italy, Spain and Portugal. It does give the grill an exotic allure. Be careful not to overcook the squid; the flesh gets rubbery. My friend Emily, who lived in Portugal and sent me scenic postcards from the countryside, contributed to this recipe.

1/2 cup olive oil
6 to 8 garlic cloves, minced
2 tablespoons minced fresh parsley
Juice of 1 lemon
1/2 teaspoon ground black pepper
1/2 teaspoon salt
1 pound squid, cleaned
1 head red or green leaf lettuce, rinsed
2 tomatoes, cored and chopped
1 red onion, slivered
1 cucumber, sliced
1/2 cup Dijon-style vinaigrette dressing

Combine the oil, garlic, parsley, lemon, and seasonings in a mixing bowl and whisk well. Place the squid in the mixture and chill for 2 to 3 hours.

Form the salad with the lettuce, tomatoes, onion, cucumber, and vinaigrette.

Preheat the grill until the coals are gray to white.

When the fire is ready, remove the squid from the marinade and place on the oiled grill. Cook for 5 to 7 minutes on each side, until firm and cooked in the center. Serve over the tossed salads with Portuguese or French bread on the side.

Yield: 4 servings

Soft-Shell Crab Sandwiches with Lemon-Dill Basting Sauce

USA

Soft-shell crab sandwiches are the best. In the late spring and early summer, whenever I visit the East Coast corridor—Washington, Boston, New York—I seek out the freshest fish markets in search of soft-shell crabs. They are especially a treat when grilled over a low open fire. Soft-shell crabs should be basted frequently with the sauce.

1/2 cup lemon juice
1/4 cup melted butter
2 tablespoons Worcestershire sauce
2 tablespoons minced fresh dill
1/2 teaspoon ground black pepper
1/2 teaspoon salt
4 to 6 soft-shell crabs, cleaned
1 large loaf French bread
1 head green leaf lettuce, cleaned
2 tomatoes, cored and sliced

To make the basting sauce, combine all of the ingredients (except the crabs) in a mixing bowl and whisk well. Set aside and keep warm.

Preheat the grill until the coals are gray to white.

When the fire is ready, place the crabs on the oiled grill. Cook each side for 5 to 7 minutes, basting frequently.

Slice the bread in half and warm it on the grill. When the crabs are cooked on the inside, assemble sandwiches with the crab, lettuce, and tomatoes. Mayonnaise is optional.

Yield: 4 servings

Swordfish Souvlaki with Mesclun and Feta Salad

GREECE

The meaty texture and strong flavor of swordfish is a natural for the herbal flavors of souvlaki. Serving the fish with mesclun (a mixture of leafy greens and vegetables) is a healthful and flavorful variation. Mesclun is sold at upscale supermarkets and seasonal farmer's markets. You can make your own mesclun salad with a combination of red and green leaf lettuce, mustard greens, arugula, kale, beet greens, and just about any other leafy vegetables. The presence of feta is in keeping with the Greek theme.

For the souvlaki:

1/2 cup olive oil
1/4 cup lemon juice
4 garlic cloves, minced
1 tablespoon dried oregano
1 tablespoon fresh thyme leaves or
  1 1/2 teaspoons dried
1 teaspoon ground black pepper
1/2 teaspoon salt
1 1/2 pounds swordfish or marlin steaks,
  cut into 2-inch cubes

For the salad:

1 pound mesclun, or salad of mixed leafy
  greens
1/3 pound crumbled feta cheese
1 large red onion, quartered
1 summer squash, coarsely chopped
8 to 12 cherry tomatoes
2 lemons, quartered
4 pita breads, warmed on the grill

Combine all of the souvlaki ingredients (except the fish) in a mixing bowl and whisk well. Place the fish in the bowl and cover with the marinade. Chill for about 1 hour.

Meanwhile, wash the mesclun and place in a large bowl. Toss with the feta and, if you desire, a salad dressing. Chill until ready to eat.

Preheat the grill until the coals are gray to white.

When the fire is almost ready, remove the fish from the marinade. Thread onto skewers, alternating with the onion and squash. Thread the tomatoes on separate skewers. Place the skewers on the oiled grill and cook for 7 to 10 minutes, occasionally turning and basting with the remaining marinade. Remove the tomatoes before they burst and toss into the bowl of mesclun.

When the fish is opaque in the center, slide the kebabs into the bowl and squeeze the lemon over the mixture. Warm the pita on the grill and serve with the swordfish and greens.

Yield: 4 servings

Poultry
On the Grill

The growing availability of boneless chicken breasts, thighs and, more recently, turkey breasts and fillets, have made grilled poultry more appealing than ever. The boneless cuts grill up much faster than whole parts, and have enabled a generation of cooks to appreciate grilled chicken in a matter of minutes. Pounding out the chicken and turkey pieces also expedites the grilling process.

The mild-mannered taste of poultry makes it amenable to a wide range of worldly flavors and dishes, including Jamaican Jerk Chicken, Greek Souvlaki, Thai Satay, Japanese Yakitori, Mayan Chicken with Spicy Orange Paste, and Indian Tandoori Chicken and Curry-Coated Turkey Fillets with Cilantro Raita. This chapter's poultry recipes are joined by a pantry of supporting cast members, including fresh herbs, chilies, sweet and savory spices, vinegars, wines, citrus juices, cocount milk and soy sauce.

Boneless chicken and turkey should be grilled over high heat for 12 to 15 minutes total, until it is white in the center. Whole chicken parts should be grilled over low or indirect heat for 35 to 45 minutes, until it is easily pulled from the bone. The times depend on the level of heat and distance from the coals.

Once grilled, chicken is a welcome guest at picnic tables all the world over in its myriad forms.

Chicken Yakitori
— ■ —
JAPAN

Japan's contribution to the grand culinary melting pot is not limited to sushi or sashimi. Yakitori is a grilled chicken basted with a fragrant ginger sauce. Sake (Japanese wine) is one of the main ingredients but is sometimes hard to find. However, mirin, a sweetened version of sake, can be substituted and is available in most supermarkets, usually near the soy sauce.

1/2 cup sake (Japanese wine) or mirin
1/2 cup light soy sauce
2 tablespoons minced fresh ginger
2 to 3 tablespoons sugar
1 1/2 pounds boneless, skinless chicken breasts
  or thighs, pounded and cubed
12 mushrooms
6 to 8 scallions, halved

Combine all of the ingredients (except the chicken, mushrooms and scallions) in a mixing bowl and whisk well. Dip the chicken into the marinade.

Preheat the grill until the coals are gray to white.

Thread the chicken onto skewers, alternating with the mushrooms. When the fire is ready, place the skewers on the grill and place the scallions around the edge. Baste the chicken and scallions with the marinade, turning frequently. Baste and cook for 7 to 10 minutes or until the chicken is white in the center. Remove the skewers and scallions to plates and serve with rice.

Yield: 4 servings

Tandoori Chicken with Mango Relish

INDIA

For tandoori barbecue, chicken is marinated in a fragrant and spicy yogurt marinade and roasted in a large clay pit (a tandoor oven). Tandoori chicken is characteristically an eye-catching pinkish-red in color, an effect that can be achieved by adding a few drops of food coloring to the marinade.

For this recipe, I've adapted the flavors of tandoori to the outdoor grill. Mango relish offers a fruity, sweet-and-tart juxtaposition of flavors. If you can't find mangoes, two peaches may be substituted. Stay with the Indian theme and serve basmati rice on the side.

For the marinade:
2 cups plain yogurt
1/2 cup olive oil
1/4 cup red wine vinegar
2 tablespoons minced fresh ginger root
6 to 10 garlic cloves, minced
1 1/2 tablespoons ground cumin
1 tablespoon ground coriander
1 teaspoon paprika
1 teaspoon ground clove
1 teaspoon black pepper
1 teaspoon salt
1/2 teaspoon cayenne pepper
2 drops natural red food coloring

1 1/2 pounds boneless, skinless chicken breasts, pounded and halved

For the relish:
1 ripe mango, peeled, pitted and diced
1/4 cup minced red onion
1/4 cup vegetable oil
2 tablespoons rice vinegar or red wine vinegar
2 tablespoons minced fresh mint or cilantro
Salt and black pepper, to taste

Combine all of the tandoori ingredients (except the chicken) in a mixing bowl and whisk well. Place the chicken in the marinade and marinate for 2 to 4 hours, stirring at least once.

Meanwhile, combine all of the relish ingredients in a bowl and chill.

Preheat the grill until the coals are gray to white.

When the fire is ready, remove the chicken from the marinade and place on the oiled grill. Cook for about 5 to 7 minutes on each side, until the chicken is white in the center.

Serve the chicken with mango relish and basmati rice on the side.

Yield: 4 servings

Chicken Satay with Thai Peanut Sauce

THAILAND

Thai satays have a delicate flavor with coconut overtones and an occasional flash of spiciness. Like Indonesian satays, the meal includes a peanut sauce for dipping. My favorite rice, jasmine rice, is an excellent side dish.

For the satay:
1 1/2 cups canned coconut milk
1/4 cup peanut butter
Juice of 1 lime
1/4 cup soy sauce or fish sauce
3 to 4 garlic cloves, minced
2 to 3 chili peppers, seeded and minced
2 to 3 tablespoons minced fresh cilantro
2 teaspoons ground coriander
1 teaspoon ground cumin
1 1/2 pounds boneless, skinless chicken breasts or thighs, pounded and cubed

For the peanut sauce:
1 tablespoon peanut oil
1 medium onion, diced
2 garlic cloves, minced
1 red chili pepper, seeded and minced
1/4 cup soy sauce or fish sauce
2 tablespoons lime juice
1 1/2 cups coconut milk
1 teaspoon ground coriander
1 teaspoon ground cumin
1 cup chunky peanut butter
1 tablespoon minced fresh cilantro

Combine all of the satay ingredients (except the chicken) in a mixing bowl and whisk well.

Thread the chicken onto skewers and place in a rectangular casserole dish. Pour the marinade over the skewers and chill for 2 to 4 hours. Turn the skewers after 1 hour.

Meanwhile, make the peanut sauce: Heat the oil in a skillet and add the onion, garlic, and chili. Sauté for about 4 minutes. Stir in the soy sauce, lime juice, coconut milk, coriander, and cumin. Thoroughly blend the peanut butter into the mixture. Bring the sauce to a simmer over low heat, stirring frequently. Stir in the cilantro and remove from the heat.

Preheat the grill until the coals are gray to white.

When the fire is ready, place the skewers on the grill. Turn the skewers occasionally and cook for 7 to 10 minutes or until the chicken is white in the center.

Remove the skewers to warm plates and serve with the peanut sauce and jasmine rice.

Yield: 4 servings

Chicken Spiedies with Apples and Onions

ITALY

Spiedinis, or skewers, are also known as spiedies. It is one of the few pasta-less Italian meals I ate while growing up. Spiedies have an herbal, somewhat tart flavor that is similar to the flavor of Greek souvlaki. The dish is rounded out with tart, moist grilled apples and mellow onions. I especially like to prepare this dish in autumn, when apples are at their prime in the Northeast. And grilled apples are a welcome diversion from the omnipresent apple pies and apple butter.

3/4 cup red wine vinegar
3/4 cup vegetable oil
4 garlic cloves, minced
2 tablespoons sugar
1 tablespoon dried oregano
1 tablespoon dried rosemary leaves
1 tablespoon dried basil
1 teaspoon ground thyme
1 teaspoon black pepper
1/2 teaspoon salt
1 1/2 pounds boneless, skinless chicken breasts
  and thighs
2 red apples, cored and quartered
2 red onions, quartered

Combine all of the ingredients, except the chicken, in a mixing bowl and whisk well. Add the chicken and marinate for 2 to 3 hours. Stir the marinade after 1 hour.

Preheat the grill until the coals are gray to white.

When the fire is almost ready, remove the chicken from the marinade and thread onto skewers, alternating with the apples and onions.

Place the skewers on the oiled grill and cook for 8 to 10 minutes, turning the skewers occasionally. until the chicken is white in the center. Transfer to serving plates and serve with bread.

Yield: 4 servings

Jay's Jerk Chicken

JAMAICA

Jerk means Jamaican barbecue. All vanity aside, I have spent many years in the restaurant business, and this is without a doubt one of the most popular dishes I have ever served. Its massive appeal can be attributed to the intense, well-rounded flavors—sweet, hot, herby, and spicy. I have tried many versions of jerk, both in the Caribbean and throughout this country. This recipe is still my favorite.

Scotch bonnet pepper, the fiery Jamaican chili pepper, gives authentic jerk chicken its heat. Use milder chilies like jalapeño for a toned-down version.

6 to 8 green onions, diced
1 medium size onion, diced
1 Scotch bonnet pepper (or habanero) or
  2 to 3 jalapeño peppers, seeded and minced
3/4 cup soy sauce
1/2 cup red wine vinegar
1/4 cup vegetable oil
1/4 cup brown sugar
2 tablespoons fresh thyme leaves or
  2 teaspoons dried
1/2 teaspoon ground cloves
1/2 teaspoon ground nutmeg
1/2 teaspoon ground allspice
1 1/2 pounds boneless, skinless chicken
  breasts, cut into strips

Place all of the ingredients, except the chicken, in a food processor fitted with a steel blade. Process for 10 to 15 seconds at high speed. Place the chicken in a bowl and pour the marinade over it. Refrigerate for 4 to 6 hours or overnight.

Preheat the grill until the coals are gray to white.

When the fire is ready, remove the chicken from the marinade and place on the oiled grill. Cook each side for 4 to 5 minutes, until the chicken is white in the center.

Transfer to serving plates and serve with rice and beans, Grilled Plantanos (page 99) or Island Slaw (page 95).

Yield: 4 servings

Chicken with Molho Baiano (Bahian Sauce)

BRAZIL

Bahia, located in Brazil's north country, is noted for its fiery fare, especially its *molhos*, or sauces. Bahians use a chili pepper known as *malagueta*, shaped like a cayenne pepper but similar to habanero pepper in heat. Unfortunately, malaguetas are not easy to find in the States, but your favorite hot chili will suffice. My friend Emily, who spent a year traveling in Brazil while the rest of us were in school, contributed to this recipe.

1/4 cup lime juice
2 tablespoons vegetable oil
1 tablespoon minced fresh parsley
1 tablespoon minced fresh cilantro
1 small onion, finely chopped
1 habanero or cayenne pepper, seeded and minced
1 1/2 pounds boneless, skinless chicken breast or thighs

Combine all of the ingredients, except the chicken, in a serving bowl and whisk well. Set aside.

Preheat the grill until the coals are gray to white.

Place the chicken on the oiled grill and cook for 5 to 7 minutes on each side, or until the chicken is cooked in the center. Transfer to plates and serve with *molho* (sauce) on the side. Coconut Rice and Beans (page 72) makes a good side dish.

Yield: 4 servings

Spice Island Chicken

GRENADA, ST. MARTIN

I first savored this spicy barbecued chicken on a snorkeling cruise off St. Martin, an island in the Caribbean. Nutmeg, cloves, allspice, peppercorns, and cinnamon are abundant in the Caribbean and often sold whole on the streets along with mangoes, papayas and plantains. This dish always received rave reviews as a special at my restaurant.

1 cup soy sauce
1/2 cup dark rum
1/2 cup red wine vinegar
1/2 cup vegetable oil
2 tablespoons thyme leaves
1 tablespoon minced fresh ginger
4 to 6 garlic cloves, minced
1 to 2 Scotch bonnet peppers, seeded and minced (optional)
1 teaspoon ground black pepper
1 teaspoon ground nutmeg or mace
1 teaspoon ground allspice
Juice of 1 lime
8 to 10 chicken thighs or drumsticks

Combine all of the ingredients, except the chicken, in a large bowl and whisk well. Add the chicken and refrigerate for 2 to 4 hours. Stir the marinade after 1 hour.

Preheat the grill until the coals are gray to white.

When the fire is ready, place the chicken on the oiled grill over low or indirect heat. Cover the grill, and with vents open, cook for 45 minutes to 1 hour, turning every 15 minutes. When the meat pulls easily from the bone, the chicken should be done. Serve with curried rice.

Yield: 4 servings

Chicken Souvlaki with Mint Tzatziki

GREECE

Souvlaki is grilled chicken or lamb which is heavily scented with oregano and thyme. It is served with soothing *tzatziki*, a yogurt condiment similar to Indian *raita*. For a light, healthful meal, serve the souvlaki over a bed of leafy greens and raw vegetables and offer cantaloupe for dessert.

For the souvlaki:
3/4 cup red wine vinegar
1/4 cup olive oil
1 tablespoons dried oregano
1 tablespoon fresh thyme leaves or
 1 1/2 teaspoons dried
1 teaspoon salt
1 teaspoon ground black pepper
1 1/2 pounds boneless, skinless chicken breasts
 or boneless leg of lamb, cubed

For the tzatziki:
2 cups plain yogurt
1 cucumber, peeled and grated
2 to 3 garlic cloves, minced
2 tablespoons minced fresh mint
 (or 1 tablespoon dried)
1 tablespoon red wine vinegar
1/2 teaspoon white pepper
1/2 teaspoon salt
2 red onions, quartered
2 green bell peppers, seeded and
 coarsely chopped
12 to 16 cherry tomatoes
4 pita breads, warmed

To make the souvlaki, combine the vinegar, oil, herbs, salt and pepper in a mixing bowl and whisk well. Place the chicken in the bowl and pour the marinade over it. Refrigerate for 2 to 4 hours.

To make the tzatziki, combine the yogurt, cucumber, garlic, mint, vinegar and seasonings in a mixing bowl and blend well. Chill until ready to use.

Preheat the grill until the coals are gray to white.

When the fire is almost ready, remove the chicken from the marinade. Thread onto skewers, alternating with the onions and bell peppers. Thread the cherry tomatoes on a separate skewer. Place all of the skewers on the oiled grill and cook for 7 to 10 minutes, occasionally turning, until thoroughly cooked. Remove the tomatoes before they burst.

Push the chicken and vegetables into a pita bread or over a tossed salad and serve with the tzatziki on the side.

Yield: 4 servings

Chicken with Mango-Scotch Bonnet Sauce

CARIBBEAN/YUCATAN

Mangoes are a tropical fruit with a yellow-orange flesh and smooth rind. When ripe, mangoes bring pleasure to both sweet and savory dishes, especially in chutneys, relishes, and sauces. Here it is paired with another Caribbean culinary treasure, the Scotch bonnet pepper, a pungent pod with curvaceous shape and day-glow array of colors. The sauce is a wake-up call to your palate, and smartly flavors chicken, fish and meat.

For a mild version, substitute a jalapeño for the Scotch bonnet. Whining is not allowed.

1 large ripe mango, peeled, pitted and chopped
1 medium onion, diced
1 carrot, peeled and chopped
1 to 2 Scotch bonnet or jalapeño peppers, seeded and chopped
2 garlic cloves, chopped
1 cup red wine vinegar
1/2 cup fruit juice
1/4 cup brown sugar
1/2 teaspoon salt
1/2 teaspoon ground allspice
1 1/2 pounds boneless chicken breasts, pounded out

To make the sauce, combine all of the ingredients (except the chicken) in a nonreactive sauce pan and cook over low heat, stirring occasionally. Simmer for 15 to 20 minutes, until the mixture has a thick consistency.

Allow the sauce to cool slightly and then place in a food processor fitted with a steel blade. Process for 15 to 20 seconds, until smooth. Transfer to a serving bowl.

Preheat the grill until the coals are gray to white.

When the fire is ready, place the chicken on the oiled grill. Cook for 5 to 7 minutes on each side, until the chicken is cooked in the center. Transfer to plates and spoon the sauce over the top. Serve with lots of rice. Garnish with cilantro or parsley. Refrigerate the extra sauce for another day; it will keep for several weeks.

Yield: 4 servings

Chicken with
Cornell Basting Sauce

USA

This sauce was inspired by the Cornell Barbecue Sauce, a basting sauce developed by Robert Baker, professor of food science at Cornell University. According to local lore, in the early 1950s Bob Baker developed a sauce for barbecued chicken. Over time, the popularity of the sauce grew, the recipe was passed around, and eventually it became the standard basting sauce for hundreds of roadside barbecues. In a world where uptight cooks treat their barbecue recipes like state secrets, for years the Cornell Barbecue Sauce has been actively circulated for everyone to enjoy.

My version incorporates hot sauce, paprika, and cayenne pepper into the sauce.

1 egg, beaten
1 cup vegetable oil
2 cups cider vinegar
1 to 2 tablespoons bottled hot sauce
1 tablespoon salt
1 tablespoon poultry seasoning
1/2 teaspoon ground black pepper
1 teaspoon paprika
1/4 teaspoon cayenne pepper
4 to 8 broiler halves

Beat the egg in a mixing bowl. Add the oil and beat again. Stir in the cider vinegar and all of the seasonings.

Preheat the grill until the coals are gray to white.

Push the coals to one side and place the chicken on the grate away from the coals. Cover, and with vents open, cook for about 1 hour or until drum stick easily pulls away from the flesh. Turn the chicken every 5 to 10 minutes, and baste every few minutes, lightly in the beginning and heavily near the end. Refrigerate remaining sauce for 5 to 7 days.

Serve with cole slaw, rolls and apple cider.

Yield: 4 to 8 servings

Rustic Herb Chicken with Tomato Mustard Sauce

MEDITERRANEAN

At the height of summer, I love running amok at the farmer's market and collecting as many varieties of herbs as possible. When I chop fresh herbs, the fragrance lingers on my fingertips like perfume. Herbs symbolize summer.

This marinade imbues chicken with the rustic flavors of an herb garden patch. I encourage you to try other herbs in the dish as well. The tomato mustard sauce coats the tongue with complementary tastes.

For the marinade:
1 cup vegetable oil
1/2 cup red wine vinegar
1 tablespoon Dijon-style mustard
1 tablespoon brown sugar
**1 1/2 tablespoons fresh thyme leaves or
  2 teaspoons dried**
**1 tablespoon fresh rosemary or
  2 teaspoons dried rosemary**
1 tablespoon fresh chopped basil
1 teaspoon ground black pepper
1/2 teaspoon salt

**4 (8-ounce) boneless, skinless chicken breasts,
  pounded out**

For the mustard sauce:
1 ripe tomato, cored and finely chopped
**2 tablespoons brown mustard or Dijon-style
  mustard**
1 tablespoon olive oil
1 tablespoon white wine vinegar
1 tablespoon dry white wine
Salt and pepper, to taste

Combine all of the marinade ingredients (except the chicken) in a large bowl and whisk well. Add the chicken and chill for 2 to 4 hours. Stir after 1 hour.

Combine all of the mustard ingredients in a serving bowl. Set aside.

Preheat the grill until the coals are gray to white.

When the fire is ready, remove the chicken from the marinade and place on the oiled grill. Cook for 5 to 7 minutes on each side, until the chicken is white in the center. Transfer to serving plates and serve with a few spoonfuls of mustard sauce on the side.

Yield: 4 servings

Evil Jungle Grilled Chicken with Fresh Basil

THAILAND

"Evil Jungle" refers to a Thai chicken dish flavored with coconut, lime, aromatic ingredients, and Thai curry paste. I adapted the penetrating Evil Jungle flavors to the grill, and the result was spectacular. This is a sure winner for cooks with adventurous palates.

1 tablespoon vegetable oil
4 to 6 garlic cloves, minced
2 tablespoons minced fresh ginger
2 tablespoons minced fresh lemon grass
1 to 2 tablespoons red curry or
  Panang goong paste
2 cups coconut milk
1/4 cup soy sauce or fish sauce
2 tablespoons lime juice
1 1/2 pounds boneless chicken breasts,
  pounded out and cut into wide strips
1/2 cup chopped fresh basil

Heat the oil in a skillet over medium heat and add the garlic, ginger and lemon grass. Cook for 2 to 3 minutes, stirring occasionally. Add the curry paste and cook for 1 to 2 minutes more.

Stir in the coconut milk, soy sauce, and lime juice and bring to a simmer. Remove from the heat and chill for 1 hour.

Add the chicken to the coconut-curry marinade and chill for 3 to 4 hours, stirring occasionally.

Preheat the grill until the coals are gray to white.

When the fire is ready, remove the chicken from the marinade and place on the oiled grill. Cook each side for 5 to 7 minutes, until the chicken is white in the center.

Serve on a bed of fresh basil with jasmine rice. Thai Peanut Sauce (page 28) makes a tangy side dish.

Yield: 4 servings

Rosemary Chicken with Balsamic Vinaigrette

MEDITERRANEAN

Fresh rosemary penetrates grilled chicken with a woodsy flavor and invokes the aroma of pine trees and evergreens. Balsamic vinegar, a rich, well-aged vinegar with a smooth, clean taste, provides a gentle tang to the dish.

3/4 cup vegetable oil
1/2 cup balsamic vinegar
3 to 4 garlic cloves, minced
1/2 cup fresh rosemary leaves
  (10 to 12 branches)
2 tablespoons honey
1/2 teaspoon ground black pepper
1/2 teaspoon ground nutmeg
1/2 teaspoon salt
4 (8-ounce) boneless, skinless chicken breasts,
  pounded out

Combine all of the ingredients, except the chicken, in a large bowl and whisk well. Add the chicken and marinate for 2 to 3 hours. (You may also cube the chicken before marinating and thread onto skewers.)

Preheat the grill until the coals are gray to white.

When the fire is ready, remove the chicken from the marinade and place on the oiled grill. Cook for 5 to 7 minutes on each side, until the chicken is white in the center.

Transfer to serving plates and garnish with any leftover rosemary branches. Serve with pasta.

Yield: 4 servings

Chicken Rica Rica

INDONESIA

In Indonesian parlance, rica rica roughly translates into "with a lot of spice." This is a tantalizing dish with robust flavor and golden hue.

2 tablespoons vegetable oil
4 garlic cloves, minced
1 to 2 cayenne or serrano peppers, seeded
  and minced
2 tablespoons minced shallots
2 tablespoons minced lemon grass
2 tablespoons minced ginger
2 tomatoes, cored and finely chopped
1 teaspoon salt
1/2 teaspoon turmeric or
  1 teaspoon curry powder
3 to 4 Kaffir lime leaves (optional)
1 1/2 pound boneless, skinless chicken breast
  or thighs, cut into 2-inch-wide strips

Heat the oil in large skillet or wok and add the garlic, pepper, shallots, lemon grass, and ginger. Cook over medium heat for 3 to 4 minutes, stirring frequently. Stir in the tomatoes, salt, turmeric and lime leaves and cook for about 3 minutes more. Remove from the heat and cool to room temperature.

Place the chicken in a bowl and cover with the spice paste. Chill for 2 to 4 hours or overnight. Stir the mixture after 1 hour.

Preheat the grill until the coals are gray to white.

When the fire is ready, place the chicken on the oiled grill. (You may also thread the chicken on skewers.) Cook for 5 to 7 minutes on each side, until the chicken is white in the center.

Transfer to serving plates and serve with rice or Festive Yellow Rice (page 86).

Yield: 4 servings

Lime-Peanut Chicken with Jasmine Rice

SOUTHEAST ASIA

This dish always receives rave reviews from my taste testers. The primary flavors of Southeast Asia—peanut butter, lime juice, cumin and coriander—come together to give chicken a moist texture and nutty taste.

For the marinade:

1/2 cup peanut butter
1/4 cup peanut or vegetable oil
3 tablespoons lime juice
2 tablespoons rice vinegar
2 tablespoons soy sauce
2 garlic cloves, minced
1 chili pepper, seeded and minced
1 tablespoon ground coriander
1 tablespoon ground cumin
1/2 teaspoon ground black pepper

1 1/2 pounds boneless, skinless chicken thighs or breasts, cubed
2 cups uncooked jasmine rice
4 1/4 cups water
Salt and white pepper, to taste

Combine the marinade ingredients in a mixing bowl and whisk well. Place the chicken in a bowl and cover with the marinade. Chill for 2 to 4 hours or overnight. Stir the marinade after 1 hour.

To prepare the rice, bring the water to a boil and add the rice. Cover and cook over low heat for 15 to 20 minutes, until the water is absorbed. Fluff the rice, add salt and white pepper to taste, and keep warm.

Preheat the grill until the coals are gray to white.

Remove the chicken from the marinade and place on the oiled grill. (You may also thread the chicken onto skewers). Cook for 5 to 7 minutes on each side, until the chicken is cooked in the center. Serve the chicken with the jasmine rice on the side. Garnish with a sprig of parsley or cilantro.

Yield: 4 servings

Mayan Chicken with Spicy Orange Paste

YUCATAN

In the Yucatan, the land of the Mayan culture, chicken and fish are flavored with a spicy seasoning paste called *recado* (not to be confused with Puerto Rican *recaito* or the herb *recao*). There are several variations of recado; this one emphasizes the heat.

Citrus fruits play a big role in Yucatan food, especially the bitter orange (also known as sour orange or Seville orange), which is abundantly grown there. It is almost as tart as a lemon, with a flavor similar to grapefruit. However, it is hard to find in the States, but a mixture of citrus juices can almost duplicate the flavor. Annato oil is another Yucatan ingredient that can be closely mimicked by mixing paprika and oil.

1/2 cup bitter orange juice or 1/4 cup orange juice and 1/4 cup grapefruit juice
3 to 4 garlic cloves, chopped
1 to 4 teaspoons minced habanero or jalapeño pepper
2 tablespoons chopped fresh cilantro
2 tablespoons anchiote (annato) oil (or vegetable oil combined with 1 teaspoon paprika)
1 tablespoon lime juice
1 tablespoon red wine vinegar
2 teaspoons ground cumin
2 teaspoons dried oregano
1/2 teaspoon salt
1/2 teaspoon ground black pepper
1 1/2 pounds boneless, skinless chicken breasts, cut into wide strips

Combine all of the ingredients, except the chicken, in a mixing bowl and whisk well. Add the chicken and coat entirely with the marinade. Cover and chill for 2 to 4 hours or overnight. Stir after 1 hour.

Preheat the grill until the coals are gray to white.

When the fire is ready, place the chicken on the oiled grill. Cook for 5 to 7 minutes on each side, until the chicken is white in the center. Transfer the chicken to plates and serve with beans and rice.

Yield: 4 servings

Grilled Chicken Yassa

SENEGAL

This is adapted from the Senegalese way of preparing chicken. Traditional yassa is stewed in a lemony marinade redolent with onions. The grilled version, obviously not a stew, still stays true to the spirit and flavor of yassa. Couscous, which is enjoyed in many North African countries, is a natural accompaniment.

1/2 cup lemon juice
1/4 cup peanut or vegetable oil
1/4 cup malt vinegar or red wine vinegar
1 cayenne or other chili pepper, seeded and minced
1 tablespoon fresh grated ginger
1 1/2 teaspoon dried thyme
1 teaspoon salt
1 1/2 pounds boneless, skinless chicken thighs or breasts
2 large carrots, peeled and cut into large chunks
2 medium onions, quartered

Combine the lemon juice, oil, vinegar, chili, ginger, and seasonings in a mixing bowl and blend thoroughly. Add the chicken and coat entirely with the marinade. Cover and chill for 2 to 4 hours or overnight. Stir after 1 hour.

Meanwhile, place the carrots in boiling water to cover and cook for 10 minutes. Drain and cool slightly.

Preheat the grill until the coals are gray to white.

When the fire is almost ready, alternately thread the chicken, onions, and carrots onto skewers. Place them on the oiled grill and cook for 5 to 7 minutes on each side, until the chicken is white in the center. Serve with couscous or rice.

Yield: 4 servings

Chardonnay Chicken with Savory and Marjoram

EUROPE

Classic European marinades often include dry white or red wines and aromatic herbs. The alcohol cooks off and leaves the chicken with fruity, herbal tones and heightened flavors. I like to add whole branches of savory to the marinade. Marjoram lends a subtle pine needle-like flavor.

1 cup dry Chardonnay wine
1/2 cup white wine vinegar
1/4 cup oil
2 medium onions, slivered
6 to 8 branches fresh savory
2 tablespoons fresh marjoram leaves
2 tablespoons fresh minced parsley
1/2 teaspoon ground black pepper
1/2 teaspoon salt
4 chicken quarters, rinsed

Combine all of the ingredients (except the chicken) in a large bowl and whisk well. Place the chicken in the marinade and chill for 2 to 4 hours or overnight. Stir after 1 hour.

Preheat the grill until the coals are gray to white.

When the fire is ready, remove the chicken from the marinade and place on the grill. Cover the grill and cook over low or indirect heat for about 45 minutes. Turn about every 10 minutes.

When the chicken is easily pulled from the bone, remove from the heat and let stand for 5 minutes before serving.

Yield: 4 servings

Grilled Chicken with Kiwi Vinaigrette

NEW ZEALAND/CALIFORNIA

The mildly tart flavor of kiwi fruit makes it an ideal agent for vinaigrette, and adorns chicken with flair. Kiwi fruits, native to New Zealand, are oval-shaped fruits with a scruffy brown exterior and green pulp. They taste like a strawberry that has been crossed with a banana. Lo and behold, there is life for kiwi fruit after cheesecake.

3 to 4 kiwi fruits, peeled and halved
1/4 cup red wine vinegar
2 tablespoons honey
1/4 teaspoon salt
1/8 teaspoon white pepper
1/3 to 1/2 cup soybean or other vegetable oil
1 1/2 pounds boneless chicken breasts, pounded out

To make the vinaigrette, place the kiwi fruit in a food procesor fitted with a steel blade. Process for 15 to 20 seconds, forming a pulp. Add the vinegar, honey, salt and pepper and process for another 10 seconds. Slowly drizzle in the oil while the machine is running and process for another 10 seconds. Pour into a serving container and chill until ready to serve.

Preheat the grill until the coals are gray to white.

When the fire is ready, place the chicken on the oiled grill. Cook for 5 to 7 minutes on each side, until the chicken is cooked in the center. Transfer to plates and spoon the vinaigrette over the top. Serve with a tossed salad and lots of raw vegetables.

Yield: 4 servings

BBQ Duck with Piquant Plum Sauce

CHINA

The Chinese love duck. The rich flavor is often complemented with a slightly acidic plum sauce. When barbecuing duck, keep the bird away from the coals or over indirect heat; the fat drippings will cause flare-ups. Duck is best skewered on a rotisserie.

For the sauce:
4 plums, pitted and chopped
3 to 4 garlic cloves, minced
1/4 cup light soy sauce
1/4 cup orange juice
1/4 cup dry sherry or white wine
2 tablespoons rice wine vinegar
2 tablespoons sugar
1 tablespoon minced fresh ginger
1/4 teaspoon salt
1 (4 1/2 to 5-pound) duck, well rinsed and patted dry

Combine all of the ingredients (except the duck) in saucepan and bring to a simmer over medium heat. Cook for 10 to 12 minutes, stirring occasionally. Transfer the mixture to a food processor fitted with a steel blade and process for 10 to 15 seconds, until smooth. Transfer to a serving bowl and chill for 1 to 2 hours.

Preheat grill until coals are gray to white.

When the fire is ready, place the duck over low heat or indirect heat or on a spit. Cover the grill and cook for 1 1/2 to 2 hours, turning occasionally, until the duck is cooked in the center (185 degrees).

Transfer the duck to serving plates and let stand 10 minutes before carving. Serve with plum sauce.

Yield: 2 to 3 servings

Cornish Game Hens in Orange Vinaigrette

EUROPE

The first time I grilled game hens, I ended up with burnt gristle in a cup. The flame was a tad too high. By splitting the birds or roasting them on a rotisserie, I achieved dramatically improved results.

1/2 cup orange juice
1/2 cup dry white wine
1/2 cup wine vinegar
1/4 cup vegetable oil
1 medium onion, chopped
2 teaspoons dried basil
2 teaspoons dried oregano
1/2 teaspoon ground black pepper
1/2 teaspoon salt
2 Rock Cornish game hens, rinsed

Combine all of the ingredients (except the game hens) in a large bowl and whisk well.

With a sharp knife, cut the game hens in half lengthwise.

Place the birds in the marinade and chill for 2 to 4 hours.

Preheat the grill until the coals are gray to white.

When the fire is ready, remove the birds from the marinade and place on the grill. Cover the grill and cook for 25 to 30 minutes over low to medium heat. Turn about every 10 minutes.

Remove the birds from the heat and let stand for 5 minutes. Serve with chutney and rice.

Yield: 2 to 3 servings

Grilled Turkey with Cranberry Orange Chutney

NEW ENGLAND/INDIA

Chutney, an Indian relish, brings a sweet and tart sensation to the taste buds. Chutneys are traditionally prepared with mangoes, but almost any fruit can be used. Cranberries are one of my favorites. In addition to jazzing up turkey, chutney can be served with chicken, hamburgers, and steaks.

2 cups cranberries
1 medium size onion, diced
1 large apple, cored and diced
1 cup red wine vinegar
1/2 cup apple juice
1/2 cup brown sugar
1/2 cup raisins
2 garlic cloves, minced
1/2 teaspoon ground cloves
1/2 teaspoon black pepper
1/2 teaspoon salt
Zest of 1 orange (about 1 tablespoon)
2 pounds boneless turkey breast, pounded out and halved

Combine all of the ingredients (except the turkey) in a nonreactive saucepan. Cook over medium heat for about 30 minutes, stirring occasionally, until it reaches a thick consistency. Remove from the heat and transfer to a serving bowl.

Preheat the grill until the coals are gray to white.

When the fire is ready, place the turkey on the oiled grill. Cook for 7 to 10 minutes on each side, until cooked in the center. Transfer to serving plates and serve with the chutney on the side. Brown rice makes a good side dish.

Yield: 4 servings

Curry-Coated Turkey Fillets
with Cilantro Raita

INDIA

For your next Thanksgiving, put away the carving shears and gooey gravy and fire up the outdoor barby. Boneless turkey breast or fillets cook much faster than a big whole turkey baked in the oven. The Indian curry spices bring a mouthful of flavor to the dish. *Raita*, a yogurt-based condiment, is a soothing counterpart. You won't reminisce about old-fashioned turkey and gravy after this meal.

For the raita:
I cup plain yogurt
I cup finely chopped cucumber (do not peel)
1/4 cup sour cream
1/4 cup washed and chopped cilantro leaves
1/2 teaspoon ground cumin
1/4 teaspoon salt
1/4 teaspoon cayenne pepper

For the curry paste:
3 to 4 garlic cloves, minced
2 tablespoons minced shallots
I chili pepper, seeded and minced
2 teaspoons garam masala or
  ground coriander
2 teaspoons ground cumin
I teaspoon turmeric
2 1/2 tablespoons vegetable oil
I teaspoon salt

4 (6-ounce) boneless turkey fillets

Combine the raita ingredients for in a serving bowl. Chill for I hour.

Combine all of the curry paste ingredients in a mixing bowl. Dredge the turkey fillets in the spice mixture and let stand for 15 to 30 minutes.

Preheat the grill until the coals are gray to white.

When the fire is ready, place the turkey on the oiled grill. Cook for 7 to 9 minutes on each side, or until the turkey is cooked in the center.

Transfer to serving plates and serve with the raita and rice.

Cranberry Orange Chutney (page 42) can also be served.

Yield: 4 servings

Grilled Turkey with Red Chili Succotash

NATIVE AMERICAN

Succotash is a Native American dish of lima beans and corn. The crops were planted alongside each other, harvested together and cooked in a stew. The Pilgrims later added cream and butter, and other beans have been added over time. For a healthful variation with a bite, I've added red chili peppers. It makes a colorful side dish to lightly marinated turkey breast.

For the marinade:

1/2 cup vegetable oil

1/4 cup cider vinegar

1 tablespoon poultry seasoning

1/2 teaspoon ground black pepper

1/2 teaspoon salt

2 pounds boneless turkey breasts, pounded out and cut into wide strips

For the succotash:

1 tablespoon butter

1 small onion, diced

1 green or red bell pepper, seeded and diced

1 red Fresno or jalapeño pepper, seeded and minced

1 1/2 cups cooked baby green lima beans

1 cup corn kernels

1/2 teaspoon black pepper

1/2 teaspoon salt

Combine the oil, vinegar, poultry seasoning, pepper and salt in a large bowl. Place the turkey breasts in the bowl and cover with the marinade. Chill for 1 to 4 hours.

To make the succotash, heat the butter in saucepan and add the onion and peppers. Sauté for 4 minutes and then add the beans, corn, and seasonings. Cook for about 5 minutes more, stirring occasionally. Keep warm on the side of the grill.

Preheat the grill until the coals are gray to white.

When the fire is ready, remove the turkey from the marinade and place on the oiled grill. Cook for 7 to 10 minutes on each side, until cooked in the center. Transfer to serving plates and serve with the succotash on the side.

Yield: 4 servings

Seafood
On the Grill

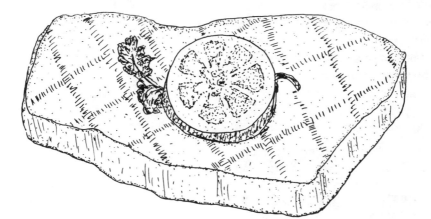

The recipes in this chapter exploit the growing penchant for grilled fish and seafood, and tap into the diverse array of sizzling fish dishes from around the world. From Jamaican Grilled Whole Red Snapper with Roasted Sweet Plantains to Indonesian Aromatic Swordfish with Coconut Marinade, Szechuan Shellfish, and Grilled Wahoo with Black Bean and Avocado Salsa, this chapter sizzles with alluring grilled seafood recipes.

Until recently, fish on the grill appeared to be reserved for upscale restaurant menus. Many home cooks had limited experience with grilled fish, and were intimidated by the prospect of a pricey fish slipping into the coals. But as the popularity and availability of fish have continued to rise, more cooks have begun to grill a variety of fish on the backyard barbecue. There's never been a better time to grill fish.

Fish with firm, dense textures, such as fresh swordfish, tuna, mako shark, mahi mahi, salmon and monkfish, are the easiest to grill. Whole fish, such as trout, red snapper, and bluefish, can be placed in a fish basket or wrapped in foil or leaves. Fillets can also be grilled, but because of varying degrees of thickness require more attention. Fish steaks can also be cubed, skewered and marinated.

For fish steaks and shellfish, it's important to start with a hot grill, since you want the fish over the heat as short a time as possible. The challenge is to sear the fish and seal in the juices. A slow-cooked fish dries out in a hurry. Whole fish, on the other hand, are best served by grilling at a lower heat. You'll find that shrimp and scallops shrink drastically on the grill, and should be skewered before grilling.

A host of marinades and spice rubs impart flavor to grilled fish. Marinaded fish should be refrigerated up to the point of grilling. It's better to skewer cubed fish and shellfish after marinating—you have to get your hands dirty but it is a more efficient use of the marinade. Salsas, relishes and sauces also adorn fish, both cosmetically and tastily. All fish and shellfish benefit from a slight brushing of oil before grilling.

The future for barbecued seafood looks bright. More and more grillable fish are showing up at the marketplace, such as wahoo, kingfish, and blue marlin. The ocean's bounty will continue to enhance your outdoor dining pleasure with a world of healthful and exotic flavors.

Blackened Catfish with Red Beans and Rice

―――■―――

CAJUN/CREOLE

"Blackened" is the Cajun practice of heavily spicing and searing fish over extremely high heat. The outside turns crusty and black and the inside remains moist. To some people, blackened spices are like salt and pepper at the table. Almost any fish can be blackened, but catfish and redfish are the authentic favorites.

Like curry powder, the seasonings are a mixture of hot and mild spices. For more heat, add more cayenne pepper; for less heat, add more chili powder, thyme, or onion powder, or cut back on the peppers. Traditionally, the fish are blackened in a skillet, but grilling adds a smoky dimension. Red beans and rice is a classic Louisiana side dish.

For the beans and rice:
2 tablespoons vegetable oil
I medium onion, diced
I green bell pepper, seeded and diced
3 to 4 cloves garlic, minced
I 1/2 cups long-grain white rice
3 cups water or vegetable stock
2 teaspoons dried oregano
I teaspoon dried thyme leaves
I teaspoon salt
1/2 teaspoon ground black pepper
2 cups cooked or canned red kidney beans

For the blackened seasonings:
I tablespoon chili powder
I 1/2 teaspoons ground black pepper
I teaspoon ground white pepper
I teaspoon paprika
1/2 teaspoon cayenne pepper
I teaspoon onion powder

I teaspoon ground thyme
2 pounds catfish or redfish fillets
2 lemons, quartered

To make the rice, heat the oil in a saucepan and add the onion, bell pepper, and garlic. Sauté for 5 to 7 minutes, until the vegetables are soft. Add the rice, water and seasonings. Cover and cook over medium heat for 10 minutes. Reduce the heat, stir in the beans, and cook for 5 to 10 minutes more, until the rice is tender. Fluff the rice and let stand.

Combine all of the blackened seasonings in a small mixing bowl. Sprinkle the seasonings over the fish, coating both sides. Store the remaining seasonings in a container with a sieve-top lid.

Preheat the grill until the coals are gray to white.

When the fire is ready, place the fish on the grill. Cook each side for 5 to 7 minutes. When the fish is opaque in the center and springs back when pressed, transfer to serving plates. Squeeze the lemon over each fish. Serve with the red beans and rice.

Yield: 4 servings

Marlin with Grilled Tomatillo Salsa

YUCATAN

Tomatillos, also known as Mexican green tomatoes, have a smooth green skin and sour flavor. They have an outer paper-like husk which slips off with the nudging of your thumb. When boiled, roasted, or uncooked, they are a staple in authentic Mexican salsas and sauces. This salsa will put you in a Yucatan frame of mind. It is spiced with the fiery habanero pepper, a culinary diamond of the Yucatan where it grows in abundance. If you prefer less heat, use a jalapeño.

Marlin is a medium-flavored, firm fish ideal for grilling. It swims in both the Pacific and the Caribbean. Swordfish is a good substitute.

For the salsa:
1 small onion, diced
2 garlic cloves, minced
Juice of 1 lime
1/2 to 1 habanero (Scotch bonnet) pepper or other chili pepper, seeded and minced
2 tablespoons minced fresh cilantro
2 tomatoes, cored and halved
6 to 8 tomatillos, husks removed and halved
1 tablespoon vegetable oil

4 (8-ounce) blue marlin or swordfish steaks
2 lemons, quartered

Combine the onion, garlic, lime juice, chili, and cilantro in a mixing bowl. Set aside

Preheat the grill until the coals are gray to white.

When the fire is ready, brush the tomatoes and tomatillos with oil and place on the grill. Cook for 4 to 6 minutes on each side. Transfer to a cutting board, chop, and combine with the onion and lime mixture. Let stand for 30 minutes at room temperature.

Place the fish on the grill and cook for 7 to 9 minutes on each side. Squeeze the lemon over the fish while it grills. When the fish are opaque in the center, remove from the grill and place on serving plates. Serve with the salsa on the side.

Yield: 4 servings

Grilled Tuna with Fig and Papaya Salsa

SOUTH AMERICAN/MEXICO

Tuna is *bonito* in South America and Mexico. Here it is adorned with a salsa of fresh figs and papayas, two abundant fruits of the regions. The combination of grilled figs and papayas in a salsa makes striking good sense once your taste buds are introduced to the pairing. It's a healthful accompaniment to grilled fish. It's a long way from fig newton.

1 ripe papaya, peeled, seeded, and chopped
2 tablespoons minced shallots
Juice of 1 lime
1 pepper or other chili pepper, seeded and minced
2 tablespoons minced fresh cilantro
1/2 teaspoon ground cumin
1/2 teaspoon salt
1/4 teaspoon ground black pepper
4 to 6 large fresh figs, halved
1 tablespoon vegetable oil
4 (8-ounce) tuna, marlin, or swordfish steaks
2 lemons, quartered

Combine the papaya, shallots, lime juice, chili, cilantro, and seasonings in a mixing bowl. Set aside.

Preheat the grill until the coals are gray to white.

When the fire is ready, brush the figs lightly with oil and place on the grill. Cook for 4 to 5 minutes on each side. Transfer to a cutting board, chop, and combine with the papaya mixture. (For a smooth salsa, transfer all of the ingredients to a food processor fitted with a steel blade and process for 10 seconds.) Place the salsa in a serving dish.

Place the fish on the grill and cook for 7 to 9 minutes on each side. Squeeze the lemon over the fish while it cooks. When the fish are opaque in the center, remove from the grill and place on serving plates. Serve with the salsa on the side.

Yield: 4 servings

Spice Rubbed Catfish with Horseradish-Cilantro Sauce

AMERICAN SOUTH

Here's a quick and easy summer meal with a splash of flavor. Catfish is too delicate for a marinade but is very accommodating to dry spice rubs and sauces. The horseradish and cilantro unite to form a sharp, clean-finishing sauce. The sauce offers a juxtaposition of flavors when eaten with the spiced catfish in the same bite. Because of catfish's texture, you don't want to micro-manage it on the grill (i.e., don't flip it too many times).

For the horseradish-cilantro sauce:
1 cup sour cream
3 to 4 tablespoons prepared horseradish
2 tablespoons minced fresh cilantro
2 tablespoons minced pimento

For the fish:
1 tablespoon chili powder
1 tablespoon ground cumin
1 teaspoon paprika
1 teaspoon ground allspice
1 teaspoon ground thyme
1 1/2 teaspoons ground black pepper
1/2 teaspoon cayenne pepper
1 teaspoon salt

1 1/2 pounds catfish or monkfish fillets

Combine the sour cream, horseradish, cilantro and pimento in a mixing bowl and whisk well. Chill for 30 minutes.

Combine all of the seasonings in a mixing bowl. Dredge the catfish in the mixture, coating both sides.

Preheat the grill until the coals are gray to white.

When the fire is ready, place the fish on the oiled grill. Cook each side for 5 to 7 minutes, until opaque in the center and it springs back when pressed.

Transfer to serving plates and spoon the sauce over the fish.

Yield: 4 servings

Greg's Trout with Tahini-Lime Sauce

MIDDLE EAST

My family tree is populated with branchloads of trout fishermen. (Not me, though—I have zero fishing prowess. The only thing I ever catch is seaweed and an occasional tree branch.) Anyway, my brother Greg, the banzai trout fisherman that he is, adapted this sauce for trout from an old Middle Eastern recipe.

Tahini is a sesame paste with the consistency of natural peanut butter. When thinned with lime or lemon juice and spices, it makes a delectable sauce for trout, black bass or other fresh water fish.

For the tahini-lime sauce:
1 cup tahini (sesame paste)
1 cup plain low-fat yogurt
3 tablespoons lime juice
1 tablespoon white wine vinegar
2 to 3 garlic cloves, minced
2 tablespoons minced fresh parsley
1/4 teaspoon salt
1/8 teaspoon cayenne

4 (8-ounce) rainbow or brown trout, dressed and deboned
1 tablespoon vegetable oil
1 tablespoon paprika
2 limes, quartered

Combine all of the sauce ingredients in a bowl and whisk well. Set aside.

Preheat the grill until the coals are gray to white.

Open the trout and baste the flesh with the oil. When the fire is ready, lay the trout flesh side down on the grill. Cook each side for 5 to 7 minutes. Sprinkle paprika lightly over the trout while the flesh side is up.

When the flesh is white in the center and flakes easily, remove the trout from the grill and place on serving plates. Squeeze the lime over the trout and serve with the tahini lime sauce on the side.

Yield: 4 servings

Coconut and
Rum Grilled Kingfish

CARIBBEAN

On my trips to the Caribbean, I avidly look forward to discovering new ways to prepare the fish. On a brief stay on Antigua I was treated to a succulent kingfish marinated in coconut and rum. Kingfish has a grayish-blue flesh with a meaty texture similar to swordfish and flavor close to sailfish. Upon my return, I recreated the dish at my restaurant and it became a popular special.

For the marinade:
2 cups canned coconut milk
1/4 cup lime juice
1/4 cup dark rum
4 cloves garlic, minced
1 tablespoon bottled habanero sauce or other hot sauce
1/2 teaspoon ground clove
1/2 teaspoon ground nutmeg
1/2 teaspoon salt

4 (8-ounce) kingfish, sailfish or swordfish steaks
2 teaspoons paprika
2 limes, quartered

Combine all of the marinade ingredients in a shallow dish and whisk well. Place the fish in the marinade and chill for 2 to 4 hours, turning the fish after 1 hour.

Preheat the grill until the coals are gray to white.

When the fire is ready, remove the fish from the marinade and place on the oiled grill. Cook each side for 5 to 7 minutes, until opaque in the center. Sprinkle the paprika over the fish while it cooks.

When the fish is done, transfer to serving plates. Squeeze the lime over the fish at the table. Serve with rice and beans and Roasted Plantains (page 108).

Yield: 4 servings

Swordfish with Mango Jicama Salsa

SOUTHWESTERN/CARIBBEAN

Here is a colorful, healthful and tasty dish that could grace the cover of the most ritzy food magazine. Two of my favorite regional cuisines, the American Southwest and the Caribbean, are fused together for one pleasurable meal. Jicama, a tan-skinned, potato-shaped vegetable with a crisp, water-chestnut texture and flavor, is juxtaposed with the fruity, smooth-rinded mango. The new wave salsa enhances the rich flavor of swordfish. Get your camera for this one.

1 large mango, peeled, pitted and diced
1 cup peeled and diced jicama
1/4 cup finely chopped red onion
1 to 3 teaspoons minced red jalapeño pepper or other chili pepper
2 tablespoons lime juice
1 tablespoon minced fresh cilantro
1/2 teaspoon salt
4 (8-ounce) swordfish, tuna or blue marlin steaks

Combine all of the ingredients, except the fish, in a mixing bowl and whisk well. Set aside for 1 hour.

Preheat the grill until the coals are gray to white.

When the fire is ready, place the fish on the oiled grill and cook each side for 5 to 7 minutes. When the fish is opaque in the center, transfer to serving plates. Serve with the salsa on the side.

Yield: 4 servings

Aromatic Swordfish with Coconut Marinade

INDONESIA

Lemon grass, ginger, turmeric and chilies characterize the culinary personality of Indonesia. The flavor print of these spices, whether in marinades, rubs or sauces, penetrates fish and chicken without crowding out the natural flavors.

Swordfish or tuna are exemplary choices for this dish. Sailfish is my choice, but it is infrequently available.

2 cups canned coconut milk
3 to 4 garlic cloves, minced
1/4 cup lime juice
2 tablespoons minced fresh lemon grass
1 tablespoon minced fresh ginger
1 to 2 chili peppers, seeded and minced
1/2 teaspoon ground turmeric
1/2 teaspoon salt
4 (8-ounce) swordfish, mahi mahi, tuna or sailfish steaks

Combine all of the ingredients (except the fish) in a casserole dish and whisk well. Place the fish in the dish and coat entirely with the marinade. Chill for 2 to 3 hours. Turn after 1 hour.

Preheat the grill until the coals are gray to white.

When the fire is ready, place the fish on the oiled grill. Cook each side for 5 to 7 minutes, until the flesh is opaque in the center and flakes easily.

Remove to serving plates and serve with Festive Yellow Rice (page 86) and garnish with the lime wedges.

Yield: 4 servings

Trout with Skordalia Sauce and Almonds

—■—

GREECE

Skordalia is the Greek answer to pesto. It is a garlicky sauce made with pureed potatoes, oil and vinegar and resembles a spiffy version of mashed potatoes. Some versions substitute trimmed bread for the potatoes, or substitute walnuts for almonds. For a lighter version, cut back on the oil and vinegar. Garnish with fresh mint or basil.

2 cups peeled, chopped all-purpose potatoes
6 to 8 garlic cloves, chopped
1/2 cup olive oil
1/4 cup red wine vinegar
1 tablespoon lemon juice
1/4 teaspoon salt
1/4 teaspoon white pepper
4 (8-ounce) rainbow trout or baby Coho
  salmon, dressed and deboned
1 tablespoon vegetable oil
1 teaspoon paprika
1/2 cup slivered almonds
2 tablespoons fresh basil or mint leaves,
  for garnish
2 lemons, quartered

To make the skordalia, place the potatoes in boiling water to cover and cook for about 20 minutes, until easily pierced with a fork. Drain and slightly cool.

Add the garlic to a food processor fitted with a steel blade and process until fine, about 10 seconds. Add the potatoes and process for 15 to 20 seconds more, until smooth. With the motor running, drizzle in the oil, vinegar, lemon juice, and seasonings and process until the sauce reaches a mayonnaise-like consistency. Transfer to a serving bowl and keep warm.

Preheat the grill until the coals are gray to white.

When the fire is ready, open the trout and baste the flesh with the oil. Lay the trout on the grill, flesh side down. Cook each side for 5 to 7 minutes, until the flesh flakes easily and is opaque in the center. Sprinkle the paprika lightly over the trout while the flesh side is up.

Remove the trout to plates and spoon a few tablespoons of skordalia sauce over each fish. Sprinkle with almonds and herbs. Squeeze the lemon over the trout and pass the extra sauce at the table.

Yield: 4 servings

Bajan Mako Shark with Chopped Seasoning

BARBADOS

"Chopped seasoning" is a blend of spices and herbs used to flavor the food of Barbados, especially fried flying fish, the Bajan national dish. Unfortunately, you can't find flying fish in the States, but mako shark, another popular Bajan fish, is available at many fish markets. Mako shark has the texture of a chewy steak, but the chopped seasoning tenderizes it while adding a surge of flavor. Monkfish also benefits from the presence of chopped seasonings.

4 to 6 green onions, chopped
1 medium onion, diced
1 Scotch bonnet pepper or jalapeño pepper,
  seeded and minced
3 to 4 cloves garlic, minced
1/2 cup vegetable oil
1/2 cup soy sauce
1/2 cup dark rum
1/4 cup lime juice
1 tablespoon fresh thyme leaves or 3 to 4
  whole thyme branches
2 to 3 tablespoons minced fresh parsley
1 teaspoon ground cloves
1/2 teaspoon freshly ground pepper
4 (8-ounce) mako shark or monkfish steaks
2 limes, quartered

Place all of the ingredients, except the fish, in a food processor fitted with a steel blade. Process for 30 seconds, forming a paste. Scrape the sides at least once during the processing.

Place the fish in a shallow bowl and coat entirely with the paste. Chill for 2 to 4 hours. Turn after 1 hour.

Preheat the grill until the coals are gray to white.

When the fire is ready, place the fish on the oiled grill.

Cook each side for 5 to 7 minutes, until the fish is opaque in the center and springs back when pressed. Transfer to serving plates and garnish with the lime wedges.

Yield: 4 servings

Grilled Whole Octopus

SPAIN, PORTUGAL, ITALY

Marinated and grilled octopus is treasured in Mediterranean countries, but Americans are a bit squeamish about it. The long tentacles give my friends the heeby-jeebies. At any rate, adventurous diners should get a real thrill out of cooking octopus on the grill. The taste and texture are very similar to squid. One note: Have the fishmonger thoroughly clean the octopus for you.

1/4 cup olive oil
1/4 cup dry sherry
1/4 cup lemon juice
4 to 6 garlic cloves, minced
1 tablespoon dried oregano
1 teaspoon paprika
1/2 teaspoon ground black pepper
1/2 teaspoon salt
1/2 teaspoon red pepper flakes
1 (1 1/2) pound octopus, cleaned

Combine all of the ingredients (except the octopus) in a mixing bowl and whisk well. Add the octopus and cover with the marinade. Chill for 2 to 3 hours. Turn after 1 hour.

Preheat the grill until the coals are gray to white.

When the fire is ready, remove the octopus from the marinade and place on the oiled grill. Cook for 7 to 9 minutes on each side, until firm and white in the center. The flesh should be slightly rubbery.

When the octopus is done, transfer to a cutting board and chop. Serve with a tossed salad or pasta.

Yield: 4 servings

Grilled Lobster Tails with Lime-Parsley Butter

CARIBBEAN/ SOUTH AMERICA

The lobsters of the Caribbean, known as spiny lobsters, have no claws. They are cherished for their meaty tails. Like their Maine cousins, spiny lobsters are best served with an herbal butter sauce.

1/4 pound butter, melted
1/4 cup minced fresh parsley
1 to 2 tablespoons lime juice
2 garlic cloves, minced
Bottled hot sauce, to taste
4 (8-ounce) lobster tails

Combine the butter, parsley, lime juice, garlic, and hot sauce in a serving bowl. Keep warm.

Preheat the grill until the coals are gray to white.

When the fire is ready, place the lobster tails on the oiled grill. Cook for 6 to 8 minutes on each side, or until the tail shell is red and the flesh is firm and white.

Transfer to a cutting board and cut the shell down the middle and extract the tail meat. Pass the sauce at the table and dip the lobster into the sauce.

Yield: 4 servings

Yellow Fin Tuna with Mango Sambal

INDONESIA

India has chutney, Mexico has salsa, and Indonesia has *sambal*. It is a sweet and hot relish served on almost every Indonesian table. The heat of a sambal is addicting—it especially brings out the flavors of grilled fish and chicken.

Although most sambals are devoted to chilies, I've created a fruity variation with tropical mangoes. If the tuna is sushi quality (meaning extremely fresh), grill the tuna to medium rare over high heat and remove it from the heat.

For the sambal:
2 tablespoons peanut or vegetable oil
1 small onion, finely chopped
2 garlic cloves, minced
2 to 3 red chili peppers, seeded and diced
1 large ripe mango, peeled, pitted and chopped
1/3 cup red wine vinegar
2 tablespoons brown sugar
1 1/2 pounds tuna, swordfish, or mahi mahi steaks
2 lemons, quartered

To make the sambal, heat the oil in a saucepan and add the onion, garlic, and chili peppers. Sauté for 5 minutes. Add the mango, vinegar, and brown sugar and cook for 15 to 20 minutes over medium heat, stirring occasionally. Remove from the heat and transfer to a food processor fitted with a steel blade. Process for 15 seconds, until smooth. Scrape into a serving bowl and chill until ready to serve.

Preheat the grill until the coals are gray to white.

When the fire is ready, place the fish on the oiled grill. Cook each side for 5 to 7 minutes, until the fish is opaque in the center. Squeeze the lemon over the fish as it grills.

Remove the fish to serving plates and serve with the mango sambal on the side.

Yield: 4 servings

Grilled Wakiki Ahi

HAWAII

Once a bastion of Spam and other imported products, Hawaiian cuisine has become a model of creativity and resourcefulness. In the past few years, Hawaiian chefs have teamed up and formed an organization called Hawaiian Regional Cuisine. Their mission is to emphasize locally grown ingredients and the abundance of locally caught seafood such as ahi, ono, opakapaka, mahi mahi, and wahoo. Many Hawaiian restaurants now rival the trendiest mainland eateries.

Ahi, the Hawaiian name for yellowfin tuna, has a burgundy red flesh with a steak-like texture. I grilled ahi near Wakiki Beach, one of the world's most famous beaches. It is available in the States as tuna.

1/2 cup orange juice
1/2 cup grapefruit juice
1/4 cup lime juice
1/2 cup dry sherry
1/4 cup soy sauce
2 tablespoons minced fresh ginger
1 to 2 tablespoons sesame oil
1/4 teaspoon cayenne pepper
1/2 teaspoon salt
4 (8-ounce) ahi (tuna), wahoo, or mahi mahi steaks
2 teaspoons paprika
2 limes, quartered

Combine the citrus juices, sherry, soy sauce, ginger, sesame oil, cayenne, and salt in a shallow baking dish and whisk well. Add the fish, cover completely with the marinade, and chill for 2 to 3 hours. Turn after 1 hour.

Preheat the grill until the coals are gray to white.

When the fire is ready, place the fish on the oiled grill. Cook each side for 5 to 7 minutes, until opaque in the center. Sprinkle the paprika over the fish while it cooks.

Remove the fish to serving plates and squeeze the lime over the top. Serve with fresh pineapple and papaya for dessert.

Yield: 4 servings

Mahi Mahi with Equatorial Guacamole

MEXICO/CARIBBEAN/PACIFIC RIM

From the South Seas to the Caribbean, mahi mahi is enjoyed for its firm flesh and mild flavor. Mahi mahi means "strong! strong!"—the yell of the Hawaiian fishermen reeling in the fish. In some parts mahi mahi is known as dolphinfish, but it is not related to dolphin, the swimming mammal.

The accompanying guacamole is a tropical spin on the classic Mexican dip. It encompasses the flavors of the equator. "Pass the guac" is a refrain I hear when I make this condiment. Have some tortillas handy to finish the dip.

2 avocadoes, peeled, pitted and chopped
1 large tomato, cored and chopped
1 mango, peeled, pitted and chopped
2 garlic cloves, minced
1 jalapeño pepper, seeded and minced
1/4 cup pineapple juice
2 tablespoons minced shallots
1 1/2 tablespoons minced fresh cilantro
1 teaspoon ground cumin
3/4 teaspoon salt
1/2 teaspoon ground black pepper
Bottled hot sauce, to taste
1 1/2 pounds mahi mahi or monkfish fillets

Place all of the ingredients, except the fish, in a food processor fitted with a steel blade and process for 15 seconds, forming a chunky paste. Transfer to a serving bowl and chill until ready to serve.

Preheat the grill until the coals are gray to white.

When the fire is ready, place the fish on the oiled grill. Cook each side for 6 to 8 minutes, until opaque in the center.

Transfer the fish to serving plates and serve with the guacamole on the side.

Yield: 4 servings

Whole Fish with Pebre
(Chilean Hot Sauce)

CHILE

In coastal Chile, seafood is an abundant staple. Fish is often served with *pebre*, the Chilean version of *chimichuri* or salsa. It is a simple sauce with intense flavors—perfect for a mildly flavored fish in need of a flavor boost. Pebre is also a cilantro lover's dream sauce, as it has plenty of it. If cilantro gives you nightmares, try *chimichuri* sauce with the fish.

For the pebre:
5 tablespoons vegetable or olive oil
3 tablespoons red wine vinegar
1/4 cup finely chopped cilantro
1 medium onion, chopped
1 to 2 chili peppers, seeded and minced
 (jalapeño is fine)
2 garlic cloves, minced
1/2 teaspoon salt
About 1/4 cup lemon juice

2 (1 1/2 pound) whole red snappers or trout,
 scaled, gills removed, and dressed
1 teaspoon ground black pepper
1 teaspoon salt
1 lemon, quartered

Combine all of the *pebre* ingredients in a mixing bowl and blend well. Set aside for 30 minutes.

Rub the lemon juice inside the cavity and over the skin of the fish. Rub in the pepper and salt. Wrap the fish with greased aluminum foil.

Preheat the grill until the coals are gray to white.

When the fire is ready, place the fish on the grill and cook over medium heat. Cover the grill and cook each side for 8 to 10 minutes. Peek at the fish and test the inside flesh; it should be opaque and flake easily.

Transfer the fish to serving plates and unwrap the foil.

Squeeze the lemon over the fish and serve with generous amounts of *pebre* over the top.

Yield: 3 to 4 servings

Cumin Rubbed Swordfish with Couscous and Lentils

MOROCCO

When couscous is combined with lentils and vegetables, it makes a tasty and healthful side dish to grilled fish or chicken. A sprinkle of cumin and lemon enhances swordfish in a minimal but effective sort of way.

For the cous cous and lentils:

1 cup brown or red lentils, rinsed
2 tablespoons vegetable oil
1 small onion, diced
1 small red or green bell pepper, seeded and diced
2 garlic cloves, minced
1 jalapeño pepper, seeded and minced (optional)
1 tablespoon minced fresh cilantro
1 teaspoon chili powder
1/2 teaspoon ground black pepper
1/2 teaspoon salt
1 cup couscous

For the fish:

1 tablespoon ground cumin
4 (8-ounce) swordfish or blue marlin steaks
2 lemons, quartered

Place the lentils in about 5 cups of water and cook for 45 minutes over medium heat, until tender. Drain and reserve about 1 cup of the liquid.

Heat the oil in a saucepan and add the onion, bell pepper, garlic and chili. Saute for 7 minutes. Add the lentils, cooking liquid, and seasonings and simmer for 10 minutes over medium heat. Stir in the couscous, cover the pan, and turn off the heat. Let stand for 10 minutes. Keep warm.

Preheat the grill until the coals are gray to white.

When the fire is ready, sprinkle the cumin over both sides of the fish. Place on the oiled grill and cook for 7 to 10 minutes on each side. Squeeze a little lemon over the fish while it cooks. When the fish is opaque in the center, transfer to serving plates. Serve the couscous and lentils on the side. Garnish with lemon wedges.

Yield: 4 servings

Grilled Wahoo with Black Bean and Avocado Salsa

MEXICO/FLORIDA

What a cool name, wahoo. In the world of fish, with names like slimehead and hammerhead, wahoo is a marketing winner. Wahoo is a mildly flavored fish with a medium-firm texture—steak-like, but slightly flaky. The flavor is similar to swordfish and blue marlin. It swims off the coast of Florida and in the Pacific and the Caribbean. The accompanying black bean and avocado salsa, adapted from the classic Mexican salsa, of course, stimulates the palate without overpowering the flavor.

For the salsa:
2 cups cooked or canned black beans
1 ripe avocado, peeled, pitted and chopped
1 small onion, diced
1 large tomato, cored and chopped
2 garlic cloves, minced
1 jalapeño pepper, seeded and minced
2 tablespoons minced fresh cilantro
1 1/2 tablespoons lime juice
1 1/2 teaspoons ground cumin
1/2 teaspoon ground black pepper
1/2 teaspoon salt

For the fish:
1/4 cup lime juice
1/4 cup vegetable oil
1 teaspoon ground black pepper
4 (6 to 8-ounce) wahoo, swordfish, or tuna steaks

Combine all of the salsa ingredients in a mixing bowl and toss thoroughly. Set aside for 1 hour.

Combine the lime juice, oil, and black pepper in a shallow bowl. Place the fish in the mixture and chill for 30 minutes to 1 hour.

Preheat the grill until the coals are gray to white.

When the fire is ready, place the wahoo on the oiled grill.

Cook each side for 5 to 7 minutes, until the fish is opaque in the center and flakes easily when pressed with a fork.

Remove the wahoo to serving plates and serve with the salsa on the side. Grilled flour tortillas or pita bread completes the meal.

Yield: 4 servings

Grilled Whole Red Snapper with Roasted Sweet Plantains

JAMAICA

This Jamaican way of cooking fish is healthful, easy, and most of all, flavorful without a lot of fuss. Just season the fish, wrap it in banana leaves or foil, and place the whole thing on the grill. For an herbal twist, place whole branches of fresh thyme or rosemary inside the fish cavity before roasting. If eating a fish with its head still intact gives you the creeps, ask the butcher to remove it. The plantains are an appealing side dish. Two Jamaican friends of mine, Claire and Michele Terrelonge, contributed to this recipe.

4 (1 1/2 pound) whole red snappers, scaled, gills removed and cleaned
1/4 cup lemon juice
1 teaspoon ground thyme
1 teaspoon ground black pepper
1 teaspoon salt
3 to 4 garlic cloves, slivered
6 to 8 branches fresh thyme or rosemary
4 yellow plantains
2 lemons, quartered

Rub the fish with the lemon juice, coating the inside cavity and the outside skin. Rub in the thyme, pepper, and salt. Place the garlic and herbs in the cavity. Wrap the fish with greased aluminum foil.

Preheat the grill until the coals are gray to white.

When the fire is ready, place the fish on the grill and cook over low to medium heat. Cut off the ends of the plantains (do not peel) and place on the grill with the fish. Cover the grill and cook each side of the fish for 8 to 10 minutes. Peek at the fish and test the flesh; it should be opaque and flake easily. Roll the plantains over every few minutes until the skin is almost black and the flesh is yellow and bulging out of the skin.

Transfer the fish to plates and unwrap the foil. Pull the plantains off the grill and make an incision into the skin and cut lengthwise. Peel away the skin and cut the plantains in half. Serve the plantains with the fish. Garnish with the lemon.

Yield: 4 servings

Salmon Steak with
Roasted Red Chili Butter

AMERICAN SOUTHWEST

Some consider the flavor of New Mexican chilies as a violin concerto when compared to the loud whistle and bells of other hot chilies. Whenever I visit New Mexico or Colorado, I load up as many chilies as I can carry back home with me. Although they are available across the country, there's a certain thrill in buying an ingredient so close to its source. During the late summer harvest, my sister Lisa sends me boxes of harvested red chilies by overnight express.

I am not in the habit of using a lot of butter in my cooking, but on rare occasions I use flavored butters to enhance grilled fish. Actually, there is just enough butter to hold the mixture together. Most of the mixture is a concentrated pulp of the red chilies.

2 fresh red New Mexican chilies
1 tablespoon minced shallots
1 tablespoon lemon juice
2 tablespoons fresh minced parsley
1 teaspoon sweet paprika
1/4 teaspoon cayenne pepper
1/4 teaspoon salt
1/2 pound butter, softened
4 (8-ounce) salmon steaks
2 lemons, cut into wedges

Make the red chili butter ahead of time. To roast the pepper, place it on an oiled grill and cook for several minutes until the skin is charred. Occasionally turn the chili. Using tongs, place the pepper in a ziplock plastic bag or rubber container with a lid and set aside for a few minutes. With a butter knife, scrape the charred skin from the flesh; discard the skin and remove the seeds.

Place the chili, shallots, lemon juice, parsley, and seasonings in a food processor fitted with a steel blade. Process for 15 to 20 seconds, forming a pulp. Scrap the sides and add the butter. Process for 15 to 20 seconds more, blending the mixture together.

Lay out a large sheet of wax paper, about a 12-inch square. Spoon the mixture onto the center of the wax paper and form a log. Roll the wax paper around the log and chill on a flat surface for 1 hour or overnight.

Preheat the grill until the coals are gray to white.

When the fire is ready, place the salmon on the oiled grill.

Cook each side for 5 to 7 minutes, until the fish is opaque in the center and flakes easily. Squirt fresh lemon over the salmon as they cook. Remove the salmon to serving plates.

Take the chili-butter out of the refrigerator. Unravel the paper and cut the log into 1/2-inch discs resembling pats of butter. Place on the center of the fish and serve at once.

The remaining butter can be refrigerated or frozen for future use. Serve the butter with Roasted Rosemary Potatoes (page 105), Barbecued Corn-on-the-Cob (page 98), or Roasted Winter Squash (page 105).

Yield: 4 servings

Grilled Salmon with Charred Red and Yellow Pepper Pesto

USA/ITALY

Lynne Sweet, a talented nutritionist and fellow celebrant of adventurous food, gave me the idea for this recipe. The robust flavor of roasted peppers combines with the garlicky aura of pesto; the result is an intensely flavored condiment well suited for a salmon or swordfish. The pesto is quite colorful and spreads like butter. Actually, I spread the remaining pesto over warm bread and it is *fabulous*.

1 red bell pepper
1 yellow bell pepper
8 to 10 garlic cloves, chopped
1/2 cup pine nuts or walnuts
1 cup packed fresh basil leaves
1/4 cup olive oil
1/2 teaspoon ground black pepper
1/2 teaspoon salt
1/3 cup grated Parmesan or Romano cheese
4 (8-ounce) salmon or swordfish steaks
2 lemons, cut into wedges

Preheat the grill until the coals are gray to white.

When the fire is ready, place the peppers on the grill and cook for 7 to 10 minutes on each side, until the outside skin is charred. Remove from the heat and let cool. Place into a ziplock plastic bag or rubber container and seal. After a few minutes, scrape off the charred skin with a butter knife. Remove the seeds and coarsely chop the flesh.

Add the garlic and nuts to a food processor fitted with a steel blade and process for 15 seconds. Add the peppers, basil, oil and seasonings and process for 10 to 15 seconds more, until a thick paste is formed. Transfer to a serving bowl and blend in the cheese. Chill until ready to serve. (The pesto can be made ahead of time.)

Heat up the grill again. When the fire is ready, place the fish on the grill and cook each side for 5 to 7 minutes. Squeeze the lemon over the fish as it cooks. When the fish is opaque in the center, transfer to serving plates. With a melon ball scooper, scoop the pesto and place on top of the fish. Spread the extra pesto over warm bread or Roasted Rosemary Potatoes (page 105) or Roasted Winter Squash (page 105).

Yield: 4 servings

Salmon with Tropical Fruit Salsa

CARIBBEAN/MEXICO

The delicate flavor and inviting pink hue of salmon make it a grilling favorite. Although many chefs serve salmon with rich sauces such as hollandaise or bernaise, I prefer to serve a fruity, palate-cleansing salsa. I would also like to add that hollandaise is the most overrated sauce in the history of food, but that's another story.

For the salsa:
2 cups chopped pineapple
4 kiwis, peeled and diced
1 jalapeno pepper, seeded and minced
1 tablespoon minced fresh cilantro
Juice of 1 lime
1/2 teaspoon salt

For the fish:
4 (8-ounce) salmon or swordfish steaks
1 to 2 tablespoons vegetable oil
2 teaspoons ground cumin
2 limes or lemon, quartered

Combine all of the salsa ingredients in a bowl and mix well. Chill for 1 hour before serving.

Preheat the grill until the coals are gray to white.

When the fire is ready, lightly brush the salmon with oil and and place on the grill. Cook each side for 5 to 7 minutes, until the flesh flakes easily and springs back when pressed. Sprinkle cumin lightly over the fish while it cooks.

Remove the salmon to serving plates. Squeeze a wedge of lime over each fish and serve with the salsa.

Yield: 4 servings

Swordfish with Salsa Verde Cruda

MEXICO

Tomatilloes are as common as tomatoes in Mexican food. The natural sour bite of the tomatillo, similar to a green tomato, coaxes out the flavors of the grilled swordfish.

6 to 8 tomatilloes, husks removed
1/4 cup finely chopped red onion
1 serrano or jalapeño pepper, seeded and minced
1 tablespoon minced fresh cilantro
1/2 teaspoon ground cumin
1/2 teaspoon salt
4 (8 ounce) swordfish, tuna or blue marlin steaks

To make the salsa, place the tomatilloes in boiling water to cover and cook for 7 to 9 minutes. Drain and cool under cold running water. Chop the tomatilloes.

Add the tomatilloes, onion, chili, cilantro, and seasonings to a food processor fitted with a steel blade. Process for 10 to 15 seconds. Transfer to a serving bowl and chill for 1 hour.

Preheat the grill until the coals are gray to white.

When the fire is ready, place the fish on the oiled grill and cook each side for 5 to 7 minutes. When the fish is opaque in the center, transfer to serving plates. Serve with the salsa verde cruda on the side.

Yield: 4 servings

Turmeric Spiced Monkfish with Coconut-Mint Chutney

INDIA

Some folks refer to monkfish as "poor man's lobster" because it shares a similar texture and flavor with lobster. Well, monkfish doesn't have to wear that moniker anymore. With a little vigilance, monkfish performs admirably on the grill, and develops a flavor identity of its own. Monkfish holds up well to Indian spices and is smartly complemented with the chutney. (Chutney means "relish" in Indian phraseology.)

For the chutney:

1 cup shredded coconut
1/2 cup plain yogurt
1/4 cup finely chopped fresh mint
2 garlic cloves, minced
1 teaspoon paprika
1 teaspoon lemon juice
1/2 teaspoon salt
1/4 teaspoon cayenne pepper
1/2 teaspoon ground coriander

For the fish:

2 tablespoons lemon juice
2 tablespoons vegetable oil
1 teaspoon ground cumin
1/4 teaspoon cayenne pepper
1/2 teaspoon turmeric
1 1/2 pounds monkfish, grouper, or sea bass fillets

Combine all of the chutney ingredients in a mixing bowl and blend together. Transfer to a serving bowl and chill for 1 hour.

Combine the lemon juice, oil, cumin, cayenne pepper, and turmeric in a casserole dish. Place the fillets in the marinade and refrigerate for 30 minutes to 1 hour. Turn after 15 minutes.

Preheat the grill until the coals are gray to white.

When the fire is ready, place the fish on the oiled grill and cook each side for 6 to 9 minutes. When the fish is opaque in the center and flakes easily, transfer to serving plates. Serve with the chutney on the side.

Yield: 4 servings

Red Snapper with Green Seasoning

WEST INDIES

There is an abundance of herbs grown in the Caribbean, and many are used in seasoning pastes. Islanders from Barbados, Trinidad, Jamaica, and St. Lucia share a penchant for spicy dishes flavored with herbal seasoning pastes. This version imbues red snapper with a woodsy flavor. Any medium size whole fish may be substituted. The paste can be spread over fish steaks as well.

One of the herbs used, shadow benni (chadon beni), has a taste similar to cilantro. It's hard to find in the States; cilantro may be substituted.

1 medium onion, diced
1/2 cup white wine vinegar
1/2 cup chopped chives
1/4 cup chopped fresh cilantro
1/4 cup Shadow Benni (or parsley or cilantro)
1/4 cup chopped celery
2 to 3 garlic cloves, minced
2 tablespoons fresh thyme leaves or
   1 1/2 teaspoons dried
1 teaspoon ground black pepper
1 teaspoon salt
2 (1 1/2 pound) whole red snapper, grouper
   or trout, scaled, gills removed and cleaned

To make the seasoning paste, combine all of the ingredients (except the fish) in a food processor fitted with a steel blade. Process for 15 seconds, until smooth. Transfer to a serving bowl.

Preheat the grill until the coals are gray to white.

Spoon half of the seasoning paste into the cavity of the fish and over the top. Wrap the fish with lightly oiled aluminum foil.

When the fire is ready, place the fish on the oiled grill and cook for 8 to 10 minutes on each side. When the fish flakes easily and is opaque in the center, transfer to serving plates. Serve with the remaining seasoning paste. Roasted plantains make a good side dish.

Yield: 2 to 3 servings

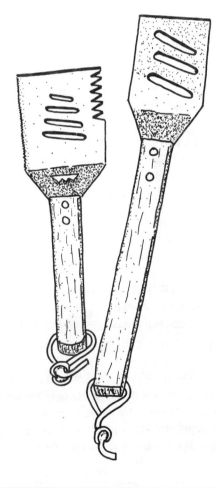

Grilled Sea Bass with Guajillo Mayonnaise

MEXICO/ FRANCE

It's a shame that guajillos are not more widely available in the States. The popular dried Mexican chilies have a mild heat and fruity, citrusy flavor. They are prominently used in salsas and sauces. I like the flavor the chili brings to homemade mayonnaise. (Mayonnaise, an American staple, is actually rooted in classical French cooking.) The chilies should be roasted and rehydrated before they are used.

Sea bass is a white, mild-tasting fish similar to halibut, and requires extra vigilance when grilling. The fish holds together well on the grill, but be careful when flipping it.

2 dried guajillo chilies or 1 ancho chili
3 pasteurized egg yolks
2 garlic cloves, minced
1 1/2 tablespoons Dijon-style mustard
1/4 cup lemon juice
1/2 teaspoon salt
1/4 teaspoon white pepper
1 1/2 cups olive or vegetable oil
4 (8-ounce) sea bass, trout, or salmon fillets
or halibut steaks

Place the chilies in a dry skillet and roast over high heat for 3 to 4 minutes. Shake the pan a few times to loosen the chilies. Then soak the chilies in hot water for about 30 minutes. Drain, remove the seeds, and mince.

To make the mayonnaise, blend the egg yolks for 15 seconds in a food processor fitted with a steel blade. Scrape the sides and add the chilies, garlic, mustard, lemon juice, and seasonings and process for another 10 seconds.

Slowly drizzle in the oil while the motor is running. When half of the oil is left, stop the processor and scrape the sides; then continue processing and drizzling. Scrape the mayonnaise into a bowl and chill until ready to serve.

Preheat the grill until the coals are gray to white.

When the fire is ready, lightly brush the fish with oil and place on the grill. Cook each side for 5 to 7 minutes, until the fish begins to flake and is opaque in the center.

Transfer the fish to serving plates and serve with the mayonnaise. Refrigerate the extra mayonnaise for later use—it will keep for 4 days in the refrigerator.

Yield: 4 servings

Fish Wrapped in Green Leaves

BALI, TAHITI, SINGAPORE

The South Seas islands share a wish-you-were-here beaches and balmy climate, and also similar cooking styles. Islanders typically season the bounty of fish with a spicy paste, wrap it in fibrous banana leaves and then grill it over coals. Banana leaves are hard to find, but wrapping the fish in Chinese cabbage or collard greens and then wrapping again in aluminum foil approximates the dish. As an added benefit, the greens absorb the flavors of the fish and seasonings and double as a side dish.

4 tablespoons minced shallots
4 garlic cloves, minced
1 tablespoon minced fresh ginger
1 tablespoon minced fresh lemon grass
1 to 2 red chili peppers, seeded and minced
1/2 cup catsup
1/4 cup lime juice
3 tablespoons vegetable oil
2 teaspoons ground cumin
1 teaspoon paprika
1/2 teaspoon ground turmeric
1/2 teaspoon salt
2 (1 1/2 pound) whole red or pink snappers
  or trout, scaled, cleaned, and gills removed
8 large Chinese cabbage or collard greens

Combine all of the ingredients (except the fish and cabbage) in a food processor fitted with a steel blade. Transfer to a casserole dish and coat the fish entirely with the marinade. Chill for 1 to 2 hours.

Preheat the grill until the coals are gray to white.

When the fire is almost ready, spread the greens out on a flat surface, forming two rectangles. (The leaves should overlap). Place the fish in the center of the leaves, include as much paste as you can, and wrap the fish with the leaves. Wrap again with aluminum foil. Place the fish on the oiled grill and cook each side for 7 to 10 minutes. The flesh should be firm and opaque.

Remove the fish from the grill and unwrap the foil. Place the fish on plates and remove the greens. Chop the greens and serve on the side.

Yield: 4 servings

Teriyaki Shrimp and Pineapple Skewers

JAPAN/PACIFIC RIM

For the most part, shrimp have a mild, low-key taste. When paired with the flavors of the Pacific Rim, however, shrimp wakes up and dances on your taste buds with exuberant flavor. The size of shrimp is another matter: no matter how large they look in the store, they turn into the incredibly shrinking shrimp when cooked. The only solution is to buy large or jumbo shrimp, unless you are eating the shrimp as popcorn-like appetizers.

1/2 cup soy sauce
1/4 cup dry sherry
2 tablespoons brown sugar
2 tablespoons sesame oil
2 tablespoons lime juice
1 tablespoon minced fresh ginger
2 pounds large shrimp, peeled and deveined
2 cups cubed fresh pineapple
1 large red bell pepper, seeded and cut into chunks
2 medium onions, quartered

Combine the first 6 ingredients in a mixing bowl and whisk well. Place the shrimp in the bowl and chill for 1 hour.

Preheat the grill until the coals are gray to white.

Remove the shrimp from the marinade and alternately thread onto skewers with the pineapple, pepper, and onion.

When the fire is ready, place the skewers on the oiled grill. Cook 7 to 10 minutes, turning occasionally, until the shrimp is pink and firm in the center.

Transfer to a serving plate and serve with white rice. Season with salt and pepper at the table.

Yield: 4 servings

Scallops with Wasabi-Soy Dipping Sauce

CHINA

Wasabi is green horseradish paste commonly served with sushi and sashimi. By itself, wasabi conducts a nose-tingling, pungent, unrelenting assault on the senses. But when wasabi is combined with soy sauce and spices, the effect is tempered, and the resulting flavors are enjoyable in yet another way.

2 tablespoons wasabi powder (available where Asian foods are sold)
2 tablespoons water
1/2 cup soy sauce
1 tablespoon vegetable oil
1 tablespoon lime juice
1 tablespoon minced fresh ginger
1 teaspoon cornstarch
1 teaspoon warm water
1 1/2 pounds large sea scallops, rinsed

Combine the wasabi powder and water to form a paste. Let stand for 5 minutes.

To make the sauce, combine the wasabi paste, soy sauce, oil, lime juice, and ginger in a saucepan. Bring to simmer and cook for about 7 minutes. Combine the cornstarch and warm water and whisk into the soy mixture. Heat for 2 to 3 minutes more. Transfer the sauce to a serving bowl.

Preheat the grill until the coals are gray to white.

When the fire is ready, place the scallops on the oiled grill. (You also may thread the scallops onto skewers.) Cook for 4 to 5 minutes on each side, or until opaque in the center. Transfer to serving plates and serve with the Wasabi-Soy Dipping Sauce on the side.

Yield: 4 servings

Beach Shrimp with Coconut Rice and Black Beans

BRAZIL

In Rio de Janeiro, the hub of activity revolves around the beach. Beaches are lined with "bahacas," small eateries serving a range of Brazilian food, but primarily known for a delectable skewered shrimp marinated in a lemon and garlic marinade. For those of us who can't stroll the beaches of Brazil as often as we'd like, at least we can enjoy the skewered shrimp. Coconut rice and black beans round out the meal. My traveling friend Emily Robin supplied this recipe.

For the shrimp:
1/2 cup fresh lemon juice
1/4 cup vegetable oil
1 small onion, finely chopped
4 garlic cloves, minced
1/4 teaspoon cayenne pepper
2 pounds large shrimp, peeled and deveined

For the coconut rice:
2 tablespoons vegetable oil
1 medium onion, diced
1 chili pepper, seeded and minced
1 1/2 cups uncooked long-grain rice, preferably brown
2 cups coconut milk (available in Asian and Caribbean markets)
1 cup water
1 teaspoon ground cumin
1/2 teaspoon ground black pepper
1/2 teaspoon salt
2 cups cooked or canned black beans
2 lemons, quartered

Combine the lemon juice, oil, onion, garlic and cayenne in a mixing bowl. Add the shrimp and chill for 1 to 2 hours.

To make the rice, heat the oil in a saucepan and add the onion and chili. Sauté for 5 to 7 minutes. Add the rice, coconut milk, water and seasonings, cover, and cook for 15 to 20 minutes (45 minutes for brown rice) over medium heat. Fluff the rice, stir in the beans, and keep warm.

Preheat the grill until the coals are gray to white.

When the fire is ready, remove the shrimp from the marinade and thread onto skewers. Place on the oiled grill and cook for 5 to 7 minutes, turning occasionally, until the shrimp are pink and firm.

Transfer the rice to plates and serve with the skewered shrimp in the center. Pass the lemon at the table.

Yield: 4 servings

East-West Scallops with Cilantro Aioli

JAPAN/FRANCE

Aioli is a rich, garlicky sauce with the consistency of thick mayonnaise. As an accompaniment to shellfish and fish, this classic French sauce blankets the tongue with a lush flavor and texture. I like to infuse aioli with fresh herbs such as cilantro or basil. The sauce provides a nice counterbalance to the Japanese-style grilled scallops.

For the aioli:
6 to 8 garlic cloves, chopped
1 pasteurized egg yolk
1 teaspoon Dijon-style mustard
2 tablespoons lemon juice
1/4 cup chopped fresh cilantro or basil
1/4 teaspoon salt
1/4 teaspoon cayenne
3/4 cup olive oil

For the scallops:
1/2 cup mirin (sweetened sake) or sake
1/2 cup soya or soy sauce
1/2 cup pineapple juice
2 tablespoons minced fresh ginger root
1 tablespoon sesame oil
2 tablespoons lime juice
2 teaspoons dried red pepper flakes
1 1/2 pounds large sea scallops, rinsed

To make the aioli, add the garlic to a food processor fitted with steel blade and process for 15 seconds, until minced. Add the egg yolk and process for 15 seconds more. Scrape the sides and add the mustard, lemon juice, cilantro, and seasonings; process for another 10 seconds.

Slowly drizzle in the oil while the motor is running. When half of the oil is left, stop the processor and scrape the sides; then continue processing and drizzling. Scrape the aioli into a bowl and chill.

For the scallops, combine the mirin, soy sauce, pineapple juice, ginger, sesame oil, lime juice, and red pepper flakes in a mixing bowl. Add the scallops and chill for 1 to 3 hours.

Preheat the grill until the coals are gray to white.

When the fire is ready, remove the scallops from the marinade and place on the oiled grill. (You also may thread the scallops onto skewers.) Cook for 4 to 5 minutes on each side, or until opaque in the center.

Transfer the scallops to serving plates and serve with liberal amounts of Cilantro Aioli on the side.

Yield: 4 servings

Szechuan Shellfish

— ■ —

CHINA

Szechuan, a province of China, is synonymous with spicy hot Chinese food. One of the ways to savor a Szechuan dish is to incorporate Szechuan sauce into the meal. Like hoisin sauce, Szechuan is a bit strong and achieves an optimal flavor when combined with mild ingredients, such as light soy sauce, rice wine, or sherry. Start with a quality bottled Szechuan sauce, and this dish is a winner.

1/2 cup bottled Szechuan sauce
1/4 cup light soy sauce
1/4 cup rice vinegar
1/4 cup dry sherry or rice wine
1 tablespoon minced fresh ginger
1 pound large shrimp, peeled and deveined
1 pound scallops, rinsed
1 red bell pepper, seeded and coarsely chopped
1 green pepper, seeded and coarsely chopped

Combine all of the ingredients, except the shellfish and peppers, in a large bowl and whisk well. Place the shellfish in the bowl and cover with the marinade. Chill for 1 hour.

Preheat the grill until the coals are gray to white.

When the fire is almost ready, remove the shellfish from the marinade. Thread the shrimp and bell peppers onto skewers, alternating ingredients. Scallops take longer to grill, so give them their own skewers. Place all of the skewers on the oiled grill and cook for 5 to 7 minutes on each side, or until the shrimp are pink and firm and the scallops are opaque in the center.

Transfer the skewers to serving plates and serve with rice.

Yield: 4 servings

Meat
On the Grill

It was a cave man (or cave woman) who first married fire to cooking. Roasted mastodon might have been the first barbecue.

Since then, meat has dominated the grilling scene. It has always been an easy and flavorful way to cook meat. You certainly don't need a culinary degree or advanced training, just a penchant for barbecuing.

Unfortunately, for a long time, cooks never ventured beyond hamburgers and steaks. Pick up an old cookbook and you'll see what I mean. Elmer Fudd is standing there grilling a slab of meat, plain and simple. Thankfully, that narrow, confining existence has since changed. Women are grilling as well as men, tastes have changed, and there are a variety of ways to season and embellish grilled beef, pork and lamb.

This chapter offers both traditional and innovative grilled meat dishes designed for a contemporary, healthful lifestyle. A cornucopia of spicy and herbal marinades, condiments, and spice rubs have given grilled meats new personalities. From Shish Kebabs, Argentinean Gaucho Steaks with Chimichuri Sauce, Lamb Satay with Festive Yellow Rice, Hoisin Pork with Whole Scallions, Spare Ribs with Serious Barbecue Sauce to Papaya Beefsteak with Pico de Gallo, you will find a variety of new ways to reinvigorate meat on the grill.

Here are a few practical tips. It's a good idea to trim as much fat off cuts of meat as possible. Always marinate in the refrigerator, and drain the meat completely before placing on the grill. (Oil-based marinades will cause flare-ups.) Large cuts of meat, such as spare ribs and pork butt, should either be slow cooked in the oven first or patiently barbecued over a very low heat. Steaks and cubed meats should be cooked over medium to high heat—the goal is to sear the outside and seal the juices on the inside.

For beef and lamb, the desired degree of doneness is up to you and your guests. Here is a broad guideline: Rare means pink on the inside, medium rare means a little pink, medium means a trace of pink or no pink, medium well means dark and almost dry, and well done means near the charred stage. Extremely well done means grill it until it's a hockey puck. "Pittsburgh-style" or "black and blue" means charred on the outside and raw on the inside.

After almost a decade of grilling for customers (under the auspices of pleasing them), I have learned that these definitions vary from person to person. Even the length of grilling time varies, depending upon the heat of the coals and the distance of the meat from the heat. You may want to consult your guests about how they want things cooked while you're at the grill.

Beef Fajitas with Calabacitas

AMERICAN SOUTHWEST

Fajitas evolved from efforts to make tough, flavorless cuts of beef and chicken more palatable and tender. The ingredients vary from region to region, but most marinades include lime juice, garlic and herbs. Skirt steak, a stubborn cut of beef similar to flank steak, was the original meat used for fajitas way back when.

Calabacitas are small globe-shaped summer squash with a texture similar to zucchini. Substitute yellow summer squash or zucchini if you can't find calabacita. They look nice on the grill.

For the marinade:
1/2 cup vegetable oil
1/2 cup Worcestershire sauce
1/3 cup lime juice
6 to 8 garlic cloves, minced
1 1/2 tablespoons dried oregano
1 teaspoon black pepper

For the fajitas:
1 1/2 pounds boneless flank or skirt steak or top round, cut into 2-inch-wide strips
4 calabacitas, quartered or 1 zucchini, coarsely chopped
2 medium onions, quartered
4 to 6 (6-inch) flour tortillas
2 cups shredded Monterey jack or provolone cheese
2 cups of your favorite tomato salsa

Whisk together all of the marinade ingredients. Place the beef in the marinade and chill for 2 to 4 hours, stirring after 1 hour.

Preheat the grill until the coals are gray to white.

When the fire is ready, remove the beef from the marinade and place on the oiled grill. Place the squash and onion around the edge. Grill until the beef reaches the desired degree of doneness and the vegetables are tender.

Crisp the flour tortillas by briefly throwing them on the grill and flipping them after a few seconds. To make a meal, fill the flour tortillas with the grilled meat, vegetables, cheese, and salsa. Fresh tomatoes and bell peppers are also welcome.

Yield: 4 servings

Harissa Spiced Lamb Kebabs with Minty Couscous

MOROCCO

Harissa is a spicy, cumin-scented paste used to flavor the food of Morocco. Here it gives lamb a warm, aromatic flavor. Serve the kebabs with couscous, tiny Moroccan pasta that resembles grain.

1/2 cup olive oil
1/2 cup red wine vinegar
4 garlic cloves, minced
2 tablespoons minced fresh parsley
2 to 3 tablespoons harissa (available in specialty food stores)
1 1/2 pounds boneless leg of lamb, cut into chunks
2 cups boiling water
2 cups couscous
2 tablespoons butter (optional)
2 tablespoons minced fresh mint or 1 tablespoon dried
1/2 teaspoon salt
1 large onion, coarsely chopped
1 red bell pepper, seeded and chopped

Combine the oil, vinegar, garlic, parsley, and harissa in a mixing bowl and whisk well. Add the lamb to the marinade and chill for 2 to 4 hours. Stir after 1 hour.

When you are getting ready to eat, pour boiling water over the couscous, stir in the butter, mint and salt and cover. Let stand for 5 to 10 minutes.

Preheat the grill until the coals are gray to white.

When the fire is almost ready, thread the lamb, onion, and bell pepper onto skewers, alternating the ingredients. Place the skewers on the grill and cook for 7 to 10 minutes or until the lamb reaches the desired degree of doneness. Turn the skewers every few minutes.

Remove the skewers to warm plates. Place the couscous in the center of 4 plates and slide the meat and vegetables onto the plates. Garnish with fresh mint.

Yield: 4 servings

Shish Kebabs

MIDDLE EAST

Growing up, my idea of barbecue was shish kebabs sizzling on the backyard grill. When weather permitted, my family grilled shish kebabs outdoors. As a testament to the grilling culture in my family, my grandmother gave me a set of treasured skewers that had been passed down through three generations; I have them mounted in my kitchen like a trophy.

Shish kebabs are served with homemade pita bread and *insalata* (tossed salad) and fresh corn-on-the-cob when it's in season. Tear the bread into small pieces, pinch the kebabs, and dip the whole thing into the garlicky oil mixture.

6 to 8 garlic cloves, chopped
1 cup olive oil
2 tablespoons minced fresh parsley
1/2 teaspoon ground black pepper
1/2 teaspoon salt
2 pounds boneless lamb or top sirloin, cut into
   1 1/2-inch cubes
2 medium onions, quartered
1 green pepper, seeded and chopped
1 red bell pepper, seeded and chopped
4 (8-inch) pita breads

Preheat the grill until the coals are gray to white.

Combine the garlic, oil, parsley, pepper and salt in a shallow bowl. Set aside.

Place a skewer through the center of the lamb cubes, onions, and peppers, alternating the meat with each vegetable. When the fire is ready, place the skewers on the grill. Using the pita bread, turn the skewers occasionally and cook until the meat reaches the desired degree of doneness, about 7 to 10 minutes.

Remove the skewers from the heat and slide the meat and vegetables off the skewers and into the garlic-oil mixture. Coat entirely with the garlic-oil and let stand for a few minutes. Meanwhile, warm the pita bread on the grill.

Fill the pita with the kebabs and vegetables. Serve with a tossed green salad and Hummus (page 107) or Mint Tzatziki (page 32).

Yield: 4 servings

Churrasco with Hot Pepper and Lime Sauce

BRAZIL

Barbecuing is a way of life in Brazil. *Churrasco* refers to "meat roast" in Brazil; large cuts of beef and chicken are barbecued over an open pit. When portions of the meat are done, the meat is carved off and plated and the remaining meat is returned to the fire. There is always a *molho* at the table, a lime and pepper sauce similar to salsa. I've adapted the spirit of *churrasco* to the American grill.

For the molho:
1 medium onion, finely chopped
1 to 2 chili peppers, seeded and minced
1/2 cup lime juice
2 tablespoons olive oil
2 tablespoons fresh minced cilantro
1/2 teaspoon salt

4 (10- to 12-ounce) boneless N.Y. strip or prime rib steaks, well trimmed

Combine all of the ingredients, except the beef, in a mixing bowl and chill for 1 hour.

Preheat the grill until the coals are gray to white.

When the fire is ready, place the steaks on the oiled grill. Cook until the meat reaches the desired degree of doneness.

Transfer the steaks to plates and pass the sauce around the table. Serve with rice and beans.

Yield: 4 servings

Bul Go Gi

KOREA

Next to kim chee (an odoriferous condiment with cabbage), bul go gi (pronounced "bull go gee") is Korea's best known dish. Thinly sliced meat is marinated in a fruity soy paste and then rapidly grilled over high heat. The pleasant fruity nuance is provided by Asian pears. The fruits look like rotund apples and have a pale olive skin. American pears may be substituted.

3 to 4 garlic cloves, minced
1 tablespoon minced fresh ginger
1/2 Asian pear or firm pear, cored and chopped
1/2 cup soy sauce
2 tablespoons sesame oil
2 tablespoons sugar
1 1/2 pounds top sirloin or top round, thinly sliced
6 to 8 mushrooms, halved
4 scallions, halved
1 tablespoon sesame seeds

Combine the first 6 ingredients in a food processor fitted with a steel blade (or blender) and process for 10 seconds. Pour into a large bowl and add the meat and mushrooms. Chill for 2 to 4 hours or overnight.

Preheat the grill until the coals are gray to white.

When the fire is ready, place the beef strips, mushrooms and scallions on the oiled grill. Cook for 5 to 7 minutes over high heat, or until the beef reaches the desired degree of doneness and the mushrooms and scallions are hatch-marked.

Transfer to serving plates and sprinkle with sesame seeds.

Yield: 4 servings

Steak Au Poivre with Sherry Mustard Sauce

FRANCE

Au poivre loosely means "with pepper" in French. Crushed peppercorns give meat a sharp, penetrating flavor that tingles the roof of your mouth. The sensation is soothed with the mustard sauce. It's best to use whole peppercorns and crush them yourself. A mortar and pestle does the job well, or failing that, place the peppercorns on a cutting board, cover with wax paper, and whale away with a mallet.

For the sauce:

3/4 cup light or heavy cream
1/4 cup Dijon-style mustard
2 tablespoons dry sherry or white wine
1 tablespoon fresh thyme leaves
  or 1 teaspoon dried
1/8 teaspoon white pepper
1/4 cup black peppercorns, crushed

4 (8-ounce) boneless strip steaks or rib eye
  steaks, well trimmed

Combine all of the sauce ingredients in a small bowl. Before serving, heat the sauce in a microwave until it simmers. Or place in a saucepan and cook over low heat, stirring frequently.

Combine the crushed peppercorns in a shallow dish. Firmly press the steaks into the peppercorn mixture, coating both sides. Preheat the grill until the coals are gray to white.

When the fire is ready, place the steaks on the oiled grill. Cook 5 to 7 minutes on each side, or until the meat reaches the desired degree of doneness.

Transfer the steaks to serving plates and spoon the sauce over the top. Pass the extra sauce at the table. Serve with Rosemary Roasted Potatoes (page 105) or Roasted Winter Squash (page 105).

Yield: 4 servings

Vindaloo Grilled Lamb

—■—

INDIA

Frequent patrons of Indian restaurants will recognize the term *vindaloo*. It refers to a spicy hot dish typically flavored with mustard, chilies, ginger, turmeric and cloves. Lamb, chicken, duck, and, in some regions, pork, are prepared vindaloo-style. I've adapted the flavors of vindaloo to the outdoor grill. Fragrant basmati rice makes an appealing side dish.

Vindaloo **marinade:**

4 garlic cloves, minced
2 tablespoons minced fresh ginger
1 jalapeño or other chili pepper, seeded and minced
2 tablespoons chopped fresh cilantro
1 cup low-fat yogurt
1/4 cup cider or red wine vinegar
1 tablespoon prepared mustard
1 tablespoon ground cumin
1 tablespoon paprika
1 teaspoon ground turmeric
1/2 teaspoon salt
1/2 teaspoon ground cloves

1 1/2 pounds boneless leg of lamb, cubed
1 red bell pepper, seeded and coarsely chopped
1 large red onion, coarsely chopped

Combine all of the marinade ingredients in a large mixing bowl and whisk well. Add the lamb and coat with the marinade. Chill for 2 to 4 hours or overnight. Stir after 1 hour.

Preheat the grill until the coals are gray to white.

When the fire is almost ready, alternately thread the lamb, bell pepper, and onion onto skewers. Place on the oiled grill and cook for 7 to 10 minutes, turning occasionally, until the lamb reaches the desired degree of doneness.

Serve with basmati rice and Cranberry Orange Chutney (page 42) or Apricot-Pineapple Sauce (page 85).

Yield: 4 servings

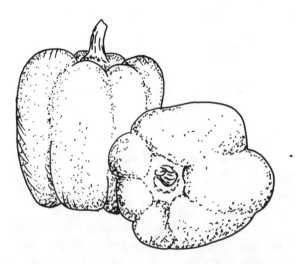

Hoisin Pork with Whole Scallions

CHINA

Hoisin sauce, by itself, is not a sauce I'd consider eating by the spoonful. But when combined with a few thinning ingredients, such as vinegar and soy sauce, the sauce emanates with savory flavors and shows off its ruby red hue.

I like to serve this dish with crunchy greens such as steamed collard greens or bok choy and brown rice. The marinade also works well with sirloin or top round steaks. Or you can use the mixture as a finishing sauce for Asian-style barbecued ribs.

1/4 cup hoisin sauce
2 tablespoons rice wine vinegar
2 tablespoons soy sauce
1 tablespoon sesame oil
4 garlic cloves, minced
1 teaspoon hot sesame oil or hot sauce
2 (8-ounce) boneless center cut pork loin
steaks or sirloin tip steaks
4 to 6 scallions

Combine the first 6 ingredients in a bowl and whisk well. Knead the pork into the marinade and chill for 2 to 3 hours.

Preheat the grill until the coals are gray to white.

When the fire is ready, remove the pork from the marinade and place on the oiled grill. Arrange the scallions around the edge of the grill. Cook the pork on each side for 5 to 7 minutes or until it is cooked in the center. Grill the scallions until tender and hatch marked. Serve the pork and scallions with brown rice and leafy green vegetables.

Yield: 4 servings

Sesame Grilled Pork

SOUTHEAST ASIA

This dish elevates pork to a sophisticated gourmet status. Lemon grass teams up with sesame oil to give pork a toasted, nutty taste and aroma. When using lemon grass, peel off the outer green layer and mince the lower, pale-green half of the stalk. Lemon grass is as integral to Southeast Asian food as garlic is to the Mediterranean cuisine and chilies are to the Caribbean.

1/2 cup soy or fish sauce
1/2 cup dry sherry or rice wine
3 to 4 garlic cloves, minced
3 tablespoons sesame oil
2 tablespoons vegetable oil
2 tablespoons minced fresh lemon grass
1 tablespoon minced fresh ginger
1 tablespoon brown sugar
1 red chili pepper, seeded and minced
1 1/2 pounds boneless pork tenderloin or
center cut loin, cubed
1 tablespoon sesame seeds

Combine all of the ingredients, except the pork and sesame seeds, in a bowl and mix thoroughly. Place the pork in the bowl and coat with the marinade. Chill for 2 to 4 hours.

Preheat the grill until the coals are gray to white.

When the fire is ready, thread the pork onto skewers and place on the oiled grill. Cook 5 to 7 minutes on each side, until the pork is cooked in the center.

Transfer to serving plates and sprinkle sesame seeds over the top. Serve with rice.

Yield: 4 servings

Lemon Grass Grilled Beef Salad with Dipping Sauce

VIETNAM

In Vietnam, grilled beef is often eaten with a salad and a salty, sweet-and-spicy dipping sauce called *nuoc cham*. A version of this dipping sauce is served at almost every Vietnamese meal.

Fish sauce, a prime flavor of this meal, is euphemistically referred to as requiring an "acquired taste." It is made from fermented fish and has an extremely pungent and salty taste. For less intense experience, but perfectly acceptable, try substituting soy sauce.

1/2 cup fish or soy sauce
3 tablespoons lemon juice
2 tablespoons minced fresh lemon grass
1/4 teaspoon cayenne pepper
1 1/2 pounds top sirloin or top round, sliced
thinly into 2-inch-wide strips

For the dipping sauce:
1/4 cup fish sauce or soy sauce
3 tablespoons rice vinegar
2 tablespoons lime juice
2 tablespoons brown sugar
1 tablespoon shredded carrots
2 garlic cloves, minced
1 red chili pepper, seeded and minced
2 tablespoons fresh mint or basil leaves
(optional)

4 tossed salads of mixed greens and vegetables
including bean sprouts, tomatoes, and
cucumbers

Combine the soy sauce, lemon juice, lemon grass, and cayenne in large bowl. Place the meat in the marinade, cover, and chill for 1 to 2 hours.

Meanwhile, combine the dipping sauce ingredients in a bowl. Set aside.

Prepare 4 tossed salads of leafy greens and vegetables. Chill until ready to eat.

Preheat the grill until the coals are gray to white.

Thread the beef onto skewers. When the fire is ready, place the skewers on the oiled grill. Grill each side for 5 to 7 minutes or until it reaches the desired degree of doneness.

When fully cooked, dip the meat into the dipping sauce and eat with the tossed salad and vegetables.

Yield: 4 servings

Pork Medallions with Apricot-Pineapple Sauce

HAWAII

The islands of Hawaii boast a plethora of tropical fruits. I've combined two of the most plentiful fruits, apricots and pineapples, to create a sweet and savory sauce perfectly suited for pork, Hawaii's favorite meat. For this dish, use pork tenderloin, which is tender and juicy. When sliced into medallions, the pork cooks quickly on the grill. The resulting meal is fruity and scrumptious. Serve another of Hawaii's bounty, passion fruit, for dessert.

1 medium onion, diced
1 cup dried apricots, chopped
1/2 cup pineapple juice
3 to 4 cloves garlic, minced
1 tablespoon minced fresh ginger
1 tablespoon Dijon-style mustard
1 cup cider vinegar
2 tablespoons Worcestershire sauce
2 tablespoons tomato puree
1/3 cup brown sugar
1 teaspoon ground black pepper
1/4 teaspoon ground allspice
1/2 teaspoon salt
2 pounds pork tenderloin, cut into 1-inch-thick medallions

To make the sauce, combine all of the ingredients (except the pork) in a saucepan. Simmer over medium heat for 20 to 25 minutes, stirring occasionally. Allow to cool, then transfer to a food processor fitted with a steel blade. Process for 15 to 20 seconds. Pour into a bowl.

Preheat the grill until the coals are gray to white.

Place the pork medallions on the oiled grill and cook each side for 6 to 8 minutes, until the pork is no longer pink in the center. Transfer to serving plates and serve with the sauce on the side.

Yield: 4 servings

Lamb Satay with Festive Yellow Rice

INDONESIA

Like the folks of the Middle Eastern and Mediterranean regions, Indonesians have a penchant for grilled lamb. Lamb satay is typically marinated in a mixture of sweetened soy sauce (ketcup manis) and sour tamarind liquid. (The liquid is derived from a dried tamarind pod which is common in Indonesia and the Caribbean but hard to find in the States. I've included vinegar as a substitute.) Ketcup manis is a sweetened version of soy sauce. Soy sauce may be substituted.

Festive Yellow Rice is traditionally served at Indonesian celebrations, such as weddings, anniversaries, and childbirths. It is scented with turmeric, coconut milk, and lemon grass and makes a warm, colorful accompaniment to satay.

For the satay:
1/2 cup ketcup manis or soy sauce
3 garlic cloves, minced
1/4 cup chopped mint leaves
2 tablespoons peanut or vegetable oil
2 tablespoons tamarind liquid or rice vinegar
2 tablespoons brown sugar
2 teaspoons ground cumin
1 teaspoon ground black pepper
1 1/2 pounds boneless leg of lamb, well trimmed and cubed

For the rice:
1 tablespoon vegetable oil
2 tablespoons minced shallots
1 tablespoon minced fresh lemon grass
1 tablespoon minced fresh ginger
1 red chili pepper, seeded and minced
1 teaspoon ground coriander
1/2 teaspoon ground turmeric
1/2 teaspoon salt
1 cup long grain rice
1 cup coconut milk
1 cup water

Combine the soy sauce, garlic, mint, oil, tamarind, brown sugar, cumin, and black pepper in a large bowl and whisk well. Add the lamb and knead into the mixture. Chill for 1 to 2 hours.

To make the rice, heat the oil in a saucepan and add the shallots, lemon grass, ginger, and chili and sauté for 3 minutes. Add the seasonings and cook for 1 minute more. Stir in the rice, coconut milk, and water and bring to a simmer over medium heat. Cover the pan and cook for 15 to 20 minutes, until the rice is tender and fluffy. Remove from the heat and keep warm.

Preheat the grill until the coals are gray to white.

When the fire is ready, thread the lamb onto skewers and place on the oiled grill. Grill the lamb until it reaches the desired degree of doneness, about 7 to 10 minutes, turning the skewers occasionally.

Transfer the kebabs to serving plates and serve with the Festive Yellow Rice on the side.

Yield: 4 servings

Gaucho Steak with Chimichuri Sauce

ARGENTINA

Gauchos are Argentinean cowboys who live off the land; to them, barbecue is what's for dinner. As a whole, Argentineans are considered barbecuing connoisseurs. They often barbecue large cuts of meat or poultry over an open pit (*asado*), similar to the *churrasco* of Brazil. *Chimichuri* (it means "spiced parsley sauce") is a vinegar-based condiment served with almost every barbecued Argentinean meal. In fact, versions of *chimichuri* can be found throughout Central and South America.

My friend Gabriella, who lived in Argentina, contributed to this recipe.

For the chimichuri sauce:
1/2 cup olive or vegetable oil
1/4 cup red wine vinegar
1 small onion, finely chopped
3 to 4 garlic cloves, minced
1 cup coarsely chopped parsley
1/2 teaspoon salt
1/2 teaspoon ground black pepper
1/8 to 1/4 teaspoon cayenne pepper

4 (12-ounce) T-bone or Porterhouse steaks, well-trimmed

Combine all of the chimichuri ingredients in a food processor fitted with a steel blade and process for 10 seconds. Transfer to a serving bowl.

Preheat the grill until the coals are gray to white.

When the fire is ready, place the steaks on the oiled grill. Cook each side for 6 to 8 minutes, until the beef reaches the desired degree of doneness.

Transfer the meat to serving plates. Spoon the chimichuri over the steaks. Pass the extra sauce at the table. I like to have flour tortillas on hand to dip into the sauce.

Yield: 4 servings

Las Vegas-Style Steaks with Pungent Horseradish Sauce

—■—

USA

My father and several cousins live in Las Vegas. Whenever I visit, they usually take me to one of the many restaurants that feature jumbo-sized steaks. Gigantic billboards announce the upcoming shows and concerts, and right below the headlining act, the daily steak special is advertised. I'm not kidding. Casinos subsidize the restaurants, so a lumberjack meal of steak and potatoes typically costs less than a hamburger elsewhere in the country. Big, juicy steaks served with a head-clearing, nose-flaring horseradish sauce. There is nothing that focuses the mind more than a jolt of the horseradish sauce—which is exactly what you need in Las Vegas.

1/2 cup sour cream
4 to 6 tablespoons high quality prepared horseradish
4 to 6 teaspoons hot sauce
4 (12-ounce) Delmonico, prime rib, or T-bone steaks, well-trimmed

Combine the sour cream, horseradish, and hot sauce in small bowl. Set aside.

Preheat the grill until the coals are gray to white.

When the fire is ready, place the steaks on the oiled grill. Cook for 5 to 7 minutes on each side, or until the beef reaches the desired degree of doneness.

Transfer the steaks to serving plates and serve with the horseradish sauce. If the sauce is too strong, blend it with more sour cream. Baked potatoes are traditionally served with this meal.

Yield: 4 servings

Thai-Grilled Beef

—■—

THAILAND

The flavors of Thailand are a fusion of pungent and aromatic spices. As a twist, I've included the barbecued flavor of Worcestershire sauce in the marinade. I like to serve the grilled meat over a tossed salad, like Rum Soaked Calypso Beef Salad (page 17). Also, Sherry Mustard Sauce (page 81) makes a contrasting condiment.

3/4 cup soy or fish sauce
1/2 cup Worcestershire sauce
1/2 cup vegetable oil
2 tablespoons lime juice
1 tablespoon minced fresh ginger
4 garlic cloves, minced
1 tablespoon sesame oil
1 tablespoon brown sugar
1 teaspoon black pepper
1 orange, quartered
1 1/2 pounds sirloin or top steak, sliced thinly into 2-inch-wide strips

Combine all of the ingredients (except the beef) in a bowl and whisk well. Squeeze the orange sections into the marinade and drop the orange sections into the mixture. Place the beef into the marinade and chill for 1 to 4 hours. Stir the marinade after 1 hour.

Preheat the grill until the coals are gray to white.

When the fire is ready, remove the meat from the marinade and place on the grill. Using tongs, turn each piece after about 2 minutes. Grill for 4 to 5 minutes or until they reach the desired degree of doneness. Serve with jasmine rice or with a tossed salad.

Yield: 4 servings

Diablo Pork with Spicy Sun-Dried Tomato Paste

SPAIN/ITALY

Diablo translates into "devil" in Spanish, which is the color of this dish. A whole brigade of red ingredients—sun-dried tomatoes, cayenne pepper, paprika, red chilies and cloves—bring a hearty, spirited flavor to pork. The sun-dried tomatoes have a robust presence. Serve the dish with red wine, naturally.

1/2 cup sun-dried tomatoes
3/4 cup vegetable oil
1/3 cup red wine vinegar
4 garlic cloves, minced
4 scallions, chopped
1 red chili pepper, seeded and minced
2 teaspoons paprika
1 teaspoon ground cloves
1 teaspoon ground thyme
1 teaspoon salt
1/4 teaspoon cayenne pepper
2 tablespoons brown sugar
1 1/2 to 2 pounds boneless pork loin or tenderloin, well-trimmed and cubed

Soak the tomatoes in warm water for 30 minutes. Drain and chop the tomatoes.

Add the tomatoes and remaining ingredients (except the pork) to a food processor fitted with a steel blade and process for 15 to 20 seconds. (The paste will still be slightly chunky.) Transfer to a large bowl. Add the pork to the bowl and cover completely with the paste. Chill for 2 to 4 hours or overnight. Stir the marinade after 1 hour.

Preheat the grill until the coals are gray to white.

When the fire is almost ready, remove the pork from the bowl and thread onto skewers. Place the skewers on the grill and cook for 7 to 10 minutes, until cooked in the center.

Remove the pork from the skewers and serve over rice.

Yield: 4 servings

Spare Ribs with
Serious Barbecue Sauce

USA

I didn't grow up in the country's barbecue belt, but I still enjoy an old-fashioned finger-licking ribs cookout once in a while. And despite several *code red* Pepto-Bismol situations, I continue to seek out barbecue shacks wherever I travel. I am in perpetual search of the ultimate barbecue experience.

I prefer to barbecue with a "finishing sauce" which is basted over the meat just before it is removed from the grill. The remaining sauce is served at the table. Try the sauce with ribs, chicken or fish. Serve it with Gusto, with a capital G.

4 to 6 pounds spare ribs (about 2 full racks)
1 large onion, finely chopped
2 garlic cloves, minced
3 tablespoons tomato paste
1 cup cider vinegar
1/2 cup apple cider
2 tablespoons brown sugar
2 tablespoons Worcestershire sauce
1 teaspoon yellow mustard
1 tablespoon molasses
1 tablespoon chili powder
1 teaspoon paprika
1 teaspoon nutmeg
1/2 teaspoon salt
1/2 teaspoon liquid smoke

You may slow cook the ribs for 2 to 3 hours over low heat in a covered cooker, or place the ribs on a baking sheet and bake at 325 degrees for 1 1/2 hours, until tender. Turn after 1 hour.

Meanwhile, combine all of the sauce ingredients in a saucepan and cook for 30 minutes over medium heat, stirring occasionally. Remove from the heat and keep warm.

Preheat the grill until the coals are gray to white.

When the fire is ready, place the baked ribs on the grill over low heat and cook for 10 to 15 minutes. Turn after 5 minutes. In the last few minutes, baste the meat with the finishing sauce.

Transfer the ribs to plates and serve with the remaining sauce at the table. Serve with Island Slaw (page 95) and rolls.

Yield: 4 servings

Spare Ribs with
Imploding Chili BBQ Sauce

—■—

USA/CARIBBEAN

This is one of those fun sauces to serve to people who love fiery food. This sweet-heat barbecue sauce will leave your mouth glowing with heat and pleasure and gastronomic comfort. The Scotch bonnet pepper delivers an intense floral heat, the chipotle pepper brings smoky heat, and the cayenne tells your tongue that the temperature is rising inside your mouth. If you have a passion for the piquant, as I do, slather this sauce over any kind of grilled food.

4 to 6 pounds spare ribs (about 2 full racks)
1 Scotch bonnet pepper or other chili, seeded
 and minced
1 medium onion, finely chopped
2 garlic cloves, minced
1/4 cup raisins
1 cup apple cider
1/2 cup cider vinegar
2 tablespoons tomato paste
2 tablespoons brown sugar
2 tablespoons Worcestershire sauce
1 chipotle or other dried chili pepper, soaked
 and seeded
1 1/2 teaspoons chili powder
1/2 teaspoon cayenne pepper
1/2 teaspoon salt
1/4 teaspoon ground allspice

You may slow cook the ribs for 2 to 3 hours over low heat in a covered cooker, or place the ribs on a baking sheet and bake at 325 degrees for 1 1/2 hours, until tender. Turn after 1 hour.

Meanwhile, combine all of the sauce ingredients in a saucepan and cook for 30 minutes over medium heat, stirring occasionally. Remove the sauce from the heat and place in a food processor fitted with a steel blade. Process for 15 seconds until smooth. Transfer to a serving dish and keep warm.

Preheat the grill until the coals are gray to white.

When the fire is ready, place the baked ribs on the grill and cook over low heat for 10 to 15 minutes. Turn after 5 minutes. In the last few minutes, baste the meat with the finishing sauce.

Transfer the ribs to plates and serve with the remaining sauce at the table. Serve with Island Slaw (page 95), rolls, and plenty of libations.

Yield: 4 servings

Papaya Beefsteak with Pico de Gallo

■━

CENTRAL AMERICA/MEXICO

Papaya, a tropical fruit with a melon-like flavor and coral flesh, has a natural enzyme that tenderizes meat. Traditional Central American and Caribbean recipes call for layering slices of papaya over tough cuts of beef and letting it marinate overnight. Pico de Gallo, alias *salsa cruda* or *salsa Mexicana*, is a blend of fresh tomatoes and chilies. It brings a bit of zip to the meal.

2 ripe papayas, peeled, seeded and chopped
1 medium onion, sliced
3 to 4 garlic cloves, minced
2 jalapeño or serrano peppers, seeded and minced
1/2 cup chopped fresh cilantro
1/4 cup vegetable oil
2 tablespoons Worcestershire sauce
1/4 teaspoon salt
4 (8-ounce) top round or top sirloin steaks, well-trimmed

For the Pico de Gallo:
2 large ripe tomatoes, cored and finely chopped
1/4 cup minced red onion
2 garlic cloves, minced
1 jalapeño pepper, seeded and minced
3 tablespoons vegetable oil
2 tablespoons red wine vinegar
2 tablespoons minced fresh cilantro
1/2 teaspoon ground cumin
1/2 teaspoon salt
1/4 teaspoon ground black pepper

Combine the papayas, onion, garlic, chili, cilantro, oil, Worcestershire sauce and salt in a shallow dish. Place the steaks in the dish and cover with the marinade. Chill for 3 to 4 hours or overnight. Turn the steaks after 2 hours.

Combine all of the Pico de Gallo ingredients in a bowl. Set aside until ready to serve.

Preheat the grill until the coals are gray to white.

When the fire is ready, place the steaks on the grill. Cook each side for 5 to 7 minutes, or until they reach the desired degree of doneness.

Transfer the steaks to serving plates and serve with the Pico de Gallo. Serve also with Bourbon-Spiked Campfire Beans (page 109) and Barbecued Corn-on-the-Cob (page 98).

Yield: 4 servings

BBQ Ribs with
Country Spice Rub

AMERICAN SOUTH

A good spice rub will give barbecued ribs a toasty crust and potent flavor, and you don't have to worry about a lot of gooey sauce running down your chin. This is just a blueprint of the basic dry rub for a down home Memphis-style barbecue. I encourage people to try different spice combinations. The spice rub can also be used on chicken and boneless pork butt.

2 tablespoons chili powder
2 tablespoons ground cumin
2 tablespoons paprika
2 tablespoons ground black pepper
2 tablespoons brown sugar
2 teaspoons salt
1 teaspoon ground allspice
1 teaspoon cayenne pepper
1/2 teaspoon ground cloves
4 to 6 pounds spare ribs (about 2 full racks)

Combine all of the spices in a bowl. Rub the mixture into the ribs. You may slow cook the ribs for 2 to 3 hours over low heat in a covered cooker, or place the ribs on a baking sheet and bake at 325 degrees for 1 1/2 hours, until tender. Turn after 1 hour.

Preheat the grill until the coals are gray to white.

When the fire is ready, place the baked ribs on the grill over low heat for 10 to 15 minutes. Turn after 5 minutes. Transfer the ribs to plates and serve with Island Slaw (page 95), Serious Barbecue Sauce (page 90) and rolls.

Yield: 4 servings

Lamb Chops with
Mint-Rosemary Sauce

EUROPE

The spring-like flavors of mint and rosemary orbit around the earthy gaminess of lamb. Sure, you can always buy mint sauce in a jar, but why not create your own delicious version? Besides, your kitchen will be filled with the inviting aroma of mint and rosemary.

1/2 cup dry red wine
1/4 cup apple cider
1/4 cup minced fresh mint
2 tablespoons fresh rosemary leaves
  or 1 tablespoon dried
2 tablespoons white wine vinegar
  or champagne vinegar
2 tablespoons confectioners' sugar
1/4 teaspoon ground black pepper
1/4 teaspoon salt
4 (6-ounce) lamb loin chops, well-trimmed

Combine all of the ingredients (except the lamb) in saucepan and bring to a simmer over medium heat. Cook for 3 to 4 minutes, stirring occasionally. Transfer to a serving bowl and chill for 1 to 2 hours.

Preheat the grill until the coals are gray to white.

When the fire is ready, place the lamb chops on the grill. Cook each side for 5 to 7 minutes, until the lamb reaches the desired degree of doneness. Transfer to serving plates and serve with the mint-rosemary sauce on the side.

Yield: 4 servings

Tikka Kebabs

—■—

AFGHANISTAN

Kebab stalls are numerous throughout Afghanistan, usually located in the town bazaars. The term *tikka* means "chunks," and is used in Afghan and Indian cooking parlance. Afghans prepare their version of kebabs with lamb, beef or minced beef. As with shish kebabs and tandoori chicken, *tikka* kebabs are served with a flat bread and fresh vegetables, such as tomatoes, onions and green vegetables.

1 1/2 cups plain yogurt
2 tablespoons lemon juice
1 small onion, grated
4 garlic cloves, minced
2 tablespoons oil
2 tablespoons grated fresh ginger
1 teaspoon ground cumin
1 teaspoon ground cardamon
1/2 teaspoon salt
1/2 teaspoon cayenne pepper
1 1/2 pounds boneless leg of lamb or sirloin steak, cubed

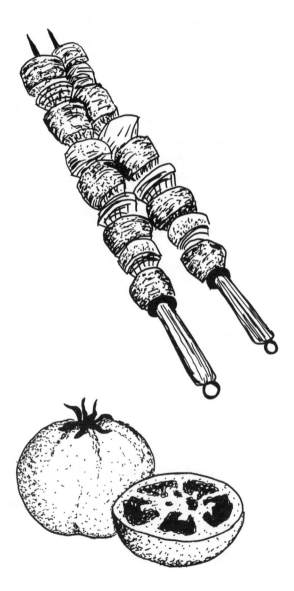

Combine all of the ingredients (except the meat) in a mixing bowl and whisk well. Add the cubed meat to the marinade and chill for 3 to 4 hours. Stir the marinade after 1 hour.

Preheat the grill until the coals are gray to white.

When the fire is ready, thread the meat onto skewers and place on the grill. Cook for 5 to 7 minutes, turning occasionally, until the meat reaches the desired degree of doneness.

Transfer the kebabs to serving plates and serve with basmati rice and fresh tomatoes and slivered onions.

Yield: 4 servings

Jerk Ribs with Island Slaw

JAMAICA

The term *jerk* is thought to be derived from the Spanish word *charqui*, which means dried meat. Another story goes that Jamaicans would jerk the slab of pork from side to side while it cooked—hence the name *jerked pork*. Using a cleaver, the jerk man hacks the jerked meat into small pieces, bones included, and piles them high in a basket.

If you don't have time to prepare an all-out jerk marinade (Jay's Jerk Chicken, page 30), this seasoning mixture might be the answer. It combines the flavors of jerk in a dry form. The spicy slaw is a perfect side dish to jerk barbecue.

2 tablespoons onion powder
2 tablespoons dried chives
1 1/2 tablespoons dried thyme
2 tablespoons brown sugar
2 teaspoons ground black pepper
2 teaspoons ground allspice
2 teaspoons salt
1 teaspoon ground nutmeg
1 teaspoon ground cloves
1/8 to 1/4 teaspoon ground Scotch bonnet
   pepper (habanero) or cayenne pepper
4 to 6 pounds spare ribs (about 2 full racks)

For the slaw:
4 cups shredded cabbage
1 cup shredded carrots
1 cup mayonnaise
2 tablespoons white wine vinegar
1 tablespoon sugar
1/2 Scotch bonnet pepper, seeded and minced
1/2 teaspoon ground black pepper
1/2 teaspoon salt
1/4 teaspoon ground allspice

Combine all of the spices in a bowl. Rub the mixture into the ribs. You may slow cook the ribs for 2 to 3 hours over low heat in a covered cooker, or place the ribs on a baking sheet and bake at 325 degrees for 1 1/2 hours, until tender. Turn after 1 hour.

Meanwhile, make the cole slaw. Combine all of the slaw ingredients in a bowl and toss thoroughly. Chill until ready to serve.

Preheat the grill until the coals are gray to white.

When the fire is ready, place the baked ribs on the grill over low heat and cook for 10 to 15 minutes. Turn after 5 minutes. Transfer the ribs to plates and serve with the slaw and rolls.

Yield: 4 servings

Vegetables
On the Grill

The sight of seasonal vegetables on the grill is a visual appetizer. Many vegetables attain a smoky flavor and texture unmatched by any kind of skillet cooking.

Tomatoes, zucchini, eggplant, onion, leeks, and sweet and hot peppers acquire heightened flavors when cooked on the grill. Winter squash and potatoes, when wrapped in foil and herbs and slow roasted, achieve unparalleled results. Grilled whole bunches of garlic come out buttery smooth. Some vegetables, such as broccoli, cauliflower, brussels sprouts, and carrots, must be precooked, but are still grillable. Corn-on-the-cob is succulent and satisfying.

The grill should be well cleaned and medium hot. Lightly basting vegetables with oil will ensure smooth turning. Vegetables should also be coarsely chopped and skewered or grilled in large sections and then chopped. Mushrooms can be left whole. Tomatoes, which cook faster than most vegetables, deserve a skewer of their own.

Many of the recipes in this chapter offer exciting ways to bring the bounty of the garden to the dinner table, via the outdoor grill. The recipes are influenced by a wide range of international dishes—some innovative, some authentic—from Grilled Vegetable Ratatouille, Yakitori Vegetables and Tofu Kebabs, Barbecued Corn-on-the-Cob, Grilled Plantanos and Roasted Winter Squash with Thyme and Allspice to Pasta al Fresco with Tomatoes, Garlic, and Squash. Vegetable dishes on the grill are sure to liven up your outdoor barbecue.

Barbecued Corn-on-the-Cob

NATIVE AMERICAN

The Indians called it *maize*. There is nothing better than the sight of fresh corn-on-the-cob roasting on the grill. Corn is the quintessential grilled food: it is grilled in its natural state, requires no namby-pamby preparations, and after it is cooked and shucked, bursts with flavor and aroma.

I have grilled corn many ways—shucked and wrapped in foil, shucked and grilled, unshucked and wrapped in foil, and so forth. My conclusion is to, first of all, start with the freshest corn possible. Then soak the corn in water, drain, and grill it, *without shucking*, in its husks. When the corn is finished, peel back the roasted husks and drink in the smoky corn aroma. Then let your teeth sink in.

4 to 6 ears of corn
Pot of cold water
Few pats of butter (optional)
Salt and pepper, to taste

Soak the corn in the water for 15 to 30 minutes. Remove from the water and pat dry.

Preheat the grill until the coals are gray to white.

When the fire is ready, place the corn on the grill. Cook over low heat for 20 to 30 minutes, turning every 5 minutes or so. Peek at the corn and check the tenderness of the kernels.

When the corn is tender, remove it from the grill and shuck off the husks. Serve with almost any grilled dish. If you desire, spread butter over the corn and season with salt and pepper. Eat at once.

Yield: 4 servings

Grilled Jalapeño Polenta with Green Tomatoes

ITALY/NATIVE AMERICAN/AFRICA/CARIBBEAN

Polenta is a dense corn meal cake which leaves you with a good taste in your mouth and a very sated feeling in your tummy. It has roots in African, Caribbean, and Native American cooking. Polenta is called funghi, coo coo, and corn meal mush, but I'd stick with polenta. Despite its recent ordination as a certified trendy dish (many chic restaurants have placed it on their menus with steep price tags), polenta is an easy and satisfying side dish.

For the polenta:
1 tablespoon vegetable or olive oil
2 1/2 cups water
1/2 teaspoon salt
1 cup yellow corn meal
1/4 cup grated Parmesan cheese
1 jalapeño pepper, seeded and minced
2 tablespoons butter, melted
2 green tomatoes, cored and sliced 1/2" thick
1 tablespoon vegetable oil

Brush an 8 1/2 x 4 1/2-inch loaf pan with the oil.

Combine the water and salt in a saucepan and bring to a boil. Gradually stir in the corn meal and cover. Cook for 12 to 15 minutes over low heat, until the polenta is thick and soft. Stir occasionally.

Stir in the Parmesan cheese, jalapeño, and melted butter, then spoon the polenta into the oiled pan. Allow the polenta to reach room temperature and then wrap and chill until ready to grill.

Invert the polenta onto a flat surface and cut into 4 sections. Brush each side of the polenta and tomato slices with the oil. Using a spatula, place the polenta and tomatoes on an oiled grill and cook for 4 to 5 minutes on each side.

Transfer the polenta sections to a plate and top with the grilled tomato slices.

Yield: 4 servings

Grilled Plantanos

WEST INDIES, SPAIN, MEXICO, CENTRAL AMERICA

Plantanos, or plantains, look like a banana on steroids. They are known as vegetable cooking bananas. When green, they resemble a potato in flavor and texture and as they ripen and turn yellow with patches of black, they become sweeter, softer, and less starchy. I prefer the flavor of ripe plantanos. They make an excellent side dish to Jay's Jerk Chicken (page 30) or Spice Island Chicken (page 31).

2 tablespoons melted butter or vegetable oil
2 yellow plantains, peeled and halved lengthwise
1/2 teaspoon ground nutmeg or allspice

Preheat the grill until the coals are gray to white.

Baste the plantain with butter and place onto the oiled grill. Sprinkle with half of the nutmeg and cook for about 5 minutes and then turn. Grill for about 5 minutes more, and sprinkle with the remaining spices. Transfer to serving plates. Serve with grilled chicken, fish, beef or vegetable dishes.

Yield: 4 servings

Grilled Fingerling Potatoes with Spiced Yogurt

TURKEY

Turkey is the land of yogurt. Unlike here, where we have to combine it with sweet fruit, the cultured milk is used in a variety of savory sauces in Turkish cuisine. As a spiced sauce, it brings flavor to fingerling potatoes. Most potatoes require long grilling times, but fingerlings, which are shaped like stubby fingers, cook in about half the time as a regular potato. Fingerlings have a natural buttery flavor.

8 fingerling potatoes, scrubbed
1 cup plain low-fat yogurt
2 teaspoons lemon juice
1 teaspoon ground cumin or coriander
1/2 teaspoon paprika
1/4 teaspoon ground cloves
1/4 teaspoon ground black pepper

Preheat the grill until the coals are gray to white.

Wrap the potatoes in greased aluminum foil. Place on the grill for 30 to 40 minutes, until tender. Turn every 15 minutes.

Meanwhile, combine the yogurt, lemon juice, and seasonings in a serving bowl. Set aside.

When the potatoes are easily pierced with a fork, peel back the foil and make an incision down the middle. Spoon the spiced yogurt over the top. Serve at once.

Yield: 4 servings

Grilled Yuca with Crushed Tomatoes and Chilies

BOLIVIA/CENTRAL AMERICA

Yuca, also known as cassava or manioc, has a waxy brown skin and starchy white flesh. The tuber is grown in South America, Central America and the Caribbean. I see people pick up yuca in the store and curiously inspect it, as if it were from another planet. Most people, however, may be familiar with yuca in another form: it is the basis of tapioca.

Although frequently fried or boiled in soups or stews, yuca can also be grilled. Here it is paired with crushed tomatoes and chilies, a favorite Bolivian condiment. Annatto oil, which has a red hue (it is derived from red annatto seeds), is basted over the yuca for color and flavor. My friend Jessica Robin, who spent several years living in Bolivia, contributed to this recipe.

2 pounds yuca
4 ripe tomatoes, cored and chopped
1 to 2 Scotch bonnet or jalapeño peppers, depending on how hot you want it
2 tablespoons annatto oil or vegetable oil

Peel the yuca and cut it lengthwise down the middle. Remove the thin rope-like center. Cut the yuca into 2-inch-wide strips. Place it in boiling water to cover and cook for 35 to 45 minutes, until easily pierced with a fork. Drain in a colander and pat dry.

Meanwhile, combine the tomatoes and chilies in a food processor fitted with steel blade or mortar and pestle. Process until mashed together and a paste is formed. Transfer to a serving bowl.

When the fire is ready, baste the yuca with oil and place on the grill. Grill for 7 to 10 minutes on each side, until tender. Serve with the tomatoes and chilies.

Yield: 4 servings

Garden Vegetables with Red Lentil Curry

INDIA

Lentil curry, or dal, is an Indian side dish. It offers sustenance and earthy curry flavors to a meal of mixed grilled vegetables. If you can't track down red lentils, use brown lentils or yellow split peas. To expedite the cooking time, soak the lentils in water for a few hours before cooking.

For the lentil curry:

1 cup dried red or brown lentils, soaked and drained
2 tablespoons vegetable oil
1 medium onion, diced
1 tomato, cored and diced
3 to 4 garlic cloves, minced
1 tablespoon minced fresh ginger
2 teaspoons Madras or Caribbean-style curry powder
1 teaspoon ground coriander or garam masala
1/2 teaspoon salt
1/2 teaspoon ground black pepper

For the vegetables:

1 yellow summer squash or zucchini, chopped
1 large red onion, chopped
2 red bell peppers, seeded and chopped
2 cups chopped eggplant

To make the lentil curry, place the lentils in 4 cups of water and cook for 45 minutes to 1 hour, until tender. Drain the lentils and reserve 2 cups of the liquid.

Heat the oil in a saucepan over medium heat and add the onion. Cook for about 5 minutes, stirring occasionally. Add the tomato, garlic, and ginger and cook for 4 to 5 minutes more. Add the seasonings and cook 1 minute more. Blend in the lentils and reserved liquid and cook for about 30 minutes, stirring occasionally. When the mixture is thick, transfer to a serving bowl and keep warm.

Preheat the grill until the coals are gray to white.

When the fire is ready, thread the vegetables onto skewers and baste with a little oil. Place on the grill and cook for 5 to 7 minutes, turning occasionally.

Spoon the lentils into the center of each plate and slide the vegetables into the center. Serve with Spiced Yogurt (page 100) or Cilantro Raita (page 43).

Yield: 4 servings

Pasta al Fresco with Tomatoes, Garlic and Squash

ITALY

This is a grilling masterpiece. The authentic flavors of Italy come through with the spirit and aroma of the great outdoors. The tomatoes burst with flavor on the grill and exude juiciness. What makes this sauce ultraspecial is the smoky flavor and buttery texture of roasted garlic. Mangia!

2 tablespoons olive oil
1 tablespoon sugar
2 to 3 tablespoons fresh basil
  or 2 teaspoons dried
1 tablespoon dried oregano
1/4 teaspoon cayenne pepper
1/2 teaspoon salt
8 to 10 large ripe tomatoes, cored and halved
1 bunch of garlic, unpeeled
1 zucchini or yellow summer squash, cut into
  long strips
1/2 pound uncooked linguini, shells or bow ties
1 cup grated Parmesan or Romano cheese
2 tablespoons minced fresh parsley

Combine the olive oil, sugar, basil, oregano, cayenne and salt in a large mixing bowl. Set aside.

Preheat the grill until the coals are gray to white.

When the fire is ready, place the tomatoes and garlic on the oiled grill. Arrange the squash around the edge. Baste with a little oil if you'd like. Grill for 7 to 10 minutes, until the tomatoes are ready to burst, the squash is tender, and the garlic is crusty brown.

Transfer the tomatoes to the oil-herb mixture and mash into the side of the bowl. For a smoother sauce, remove the remnants of the tomato skins.

Cut the squash into bite size pieces and toss with the tomato mixture. Place the garlic on a cutting board and peel. The skin should come off easily. Chop the garlic and blend into the bowl. Keep warm.

Place the pasta in boiling water to cover, stir, and return to a boil. Cook uncovered for 9 to 12 minutes, until al dente. Drain in a colander and transfer to serving plates. Spoon the grilled vegetables over the pasta and top with the cheese and parsley. Serve with warm bread.

Yield: 4 servings

Grilled Vegetable Ratatouille

―――――■―――――

MEDITERRANEAN

If you grow your own vegetables, this one is for you. Reach into the garden while the grill is heating up and pick out the juiciest specimens. The tomatoes are especially appealing when picked and sliced just before grilling. And the roasted garlic is smooth and enticing. The result is a sizzling spin on the classic Mediterranean eggplant stew.

If you are fidgety about cooking eggplant without salting it, then place it in a sieve, sprinkle with salt, and let stand for 20 minutes. This will leach out some of the bitterness. (I never notice any bitterness when it is grilled.)

2 tablespoons olive oil
2 tablespoons fresh basil, chopped,
  or 1 tablespoon dried
2 tablespoons minced fresh parsley
1 tablespoon dried oregano
1/2 teaspoon salt
1/8 to 1/4 teaspoon cayenne pepper
4 ripe tomatoes, cored and halved
1 medium onion, peeled and halved
1 green or red bell pepper, seeded and halved
1 medium unpeeled eggplant, cut into 2-inch-wide strips
1 small summer squash, cut into 2-inch-wide strips
1 small bunch of garlic, unpeeled
1/2 cup grated Parmesan or Romano cheese

Combine the oil, herbs and seasonings in a large mixing bowl. Set aside.

Preheat the grill until the coals are gray to white.

When the fire is ready, place the vegetables on the oiled grill, with the onion and garlic on the edge. Baste with a little oil if you'd like. Grill for 7 to 10 minutes, turning the veggies after about 5 minutes. When the tomatoes are ready to burst, pull them and place them in a bowl. As the other vegetables soften and develop grid marks, pull them off the grill and place them into another bowl. Remove the garlic when its skin is brown.

Transfer the tomatoes to the oil-herb mixture and mash into the side of the bowl. It's okay to discard the tomato skins, but I keep them in. Let the vegetables cool slightly and then place on a cutting board. Chop them into bite-size pieces and toss with the tomato mixture. Place the garlic on a cutting board, peel off the skin, and chop the cloves (they should be soft). Add as many cloves as you'd like, but 6 to 8 are plenty. Blend the garlic into the vegetables and, presto, you've made ratatouille. Sprinkle the cheese over the top and find some warm bread and red wine.

Yield: 4 servings

Yakitori Vegetables and Tofu Kebabs

JAPAN

My friend Marilee Murphy, who was a healthy eater long before it was fashionable, inspired this recipe. The Japanese-style marinade lends the vegetables a sharp, clean flavor without overpowering the natural taste. Tofu, when baked ahead of time, acquires a firm, taut skin and grills up wonderfully.

1 pound tofu
8 brussels sprouts
1 small broccoflower head or broccoli head, cut into florets
1/3 cup rice vinegar
1/3 cup soya or soy sauce
1/3 cup mirin (sweetened sake)
1/4 cup vegetable oil
2 tablespoons sesame oil
1 tablespoon hot sesame oil
1 tablespoon minced fresh ginger
1 tablespoon honey
1 yellow summer squash or zucchini, chopped
1 large red onion, coarsely chopped
1 red bell pepper, seeded and coarsely chopped

Cut the tofu into 1-inch cubes and place on a greased baking sheet. Bake at 375 degrees for 15 to 20 minutes, until light brown. Cool to room temperature.

Place the brussels sprouts and broccoflower in boiling water to cover and cook for about 5 minutes. Drain in a colander.

In a large bowl, combine the rice vinegar, soya sauce, mirin, vegetable oil, sesame oils, ginger and honey. Place the tofu and all of the vegetables in the bowl and marinate for 1 to 2 hours.

Preheat the grill until the coals are gray to white.

When the fire is ready, thread the vegetables and tofu onto skewers. Place on the grill and cook for 5 to 7 minutes, turning occasionally. Baste with the remaining marinade. Serve with brown rice or a green salad.

Yield: 4 servings

Roasted Winter Squash with Thyme and Allspice

NATIVE AMERICAN

Until recently, squash were considered to be big, lumpy vegetables with no place to go. The word was going around that they had a weight problem. Squash got no respect.

These days, more and more cooks are rediscovering the humble squash family. A variety of beta carotene-rich gourds, such as buttercup, acorn, calabaza, and delicata, are perfect for roasting on the grill. The subtle, sweet potato-like flavors come alive over fire. Move over, baby zucchini! Make room for roasted acorn!

2 butter cup, acorn, or delicata squash, halved
2 tablespoons cold butter (optional)
4 to 6 branches of fresh thyme
About 1/2 teaspoon ground allspice

Preheat the grill until the coals are gray to white.

With a sharp-edged spoon, remove the seedy pulp from the center of each squash. Place 1/2 tablespoon of butter in each shell and sprinkle with allspice. Place a branch of thyme in each shell. Wrap the squash in aluminum foil and place on the grill. Cook for 30 to 45 minutes over low heat, occasionally turning.

When the squash are easily pierced with a fork, remove them from the grill. Unwrap the aluminum foil and place the squash on plates. Remove the thyme branches and serve hot. They accompany any grilled dish with much aplomb.

Yield: 4 servings

Roasted Rosemary Potatoes

USA

Recently, there has been a bounty of spuds showing up at the marketplace, such as Yukon golds, purple potatoes, and fingerlings. I have found that most potatoes are good for grilling—even sweet potatoes. Wrapping the potatoes with foil keeps them moist, and including fresh herbs in the packet is a healthful way to achieve a pleasant flavor.

4 medium purple, red or Yukon gold potatoes, quartered
8 to 10 fresh rosemary branches
4 teaspoons minced garlic
1 teaspoon paprika
1/2 teaspoon ground white pepper
1/2 teaspoon salt

Preheat the grill until the coals are gray to white.

Lay out 4 sheets of aluminum foil, each 6 inches square. With a pastry brush, lightly grease the foil. In the center of each square, place 4 potato wedges, 2 or 3 branches of rosemary, and 1 teaspoon garlic. Sprinkle with the seasonings and wrap tightly. When the fire is ready, place the potatoes on the grill. Cook for 20 to 30 minutes over a medium fire, occasionally turning.

When the potatoes are easily pierced with a fork, remove them from the grill. Unwrap the foil and serve as a side dish. Spoon light sour cream or chutney over the top.

Yield: 4 servings

Pesto Grilled Vegetables

ITALY

Pesto is Genoa's gift to the world. The people of Genoa were the first to crush garlic, basil, nuts and cheese into a delicious paste. (The term is derived from "mortar and pestle.") Now pesto is omnipresent in gourmet deli salads all across the country. The quartet of ingredients delivers a perfectly pitched harmony of flavor to an array of grilled vegetables.

For the pesto:
4 garlic cloves, chopped
1/4 cup cashews or pine nuts
1 cup packed fresh basil leaves
1 cup spinach
3/4 cup olive oil
1/2 teaspoon ground black pepper
1/2 teaspoon salt
1/2 cup Parmesan cheese

For the vegetables:
8 to 10 mushrooms
10 to 12 cherry tomatoes
1 yellow zucchini or summer squash, chopped
2 bell peppers, seeded and coarsely chopped

To make the pesto, add the garlic and nuts to a food processor fitted with a steel blade. Process for 15 seconds. Add the basil, spinach, oil, and seasonings and process for 15 seconds more, until smooth. Transfer to a bowl and blend in the cheese.

Preheat the grill until the coals are gray to white.

Thread the vegetables onto skewers. (Place the tomatoes on their own skewers.) When the fire is ready, place the vegetables on the grill. Grill for 7 to 10 minutes, until tender. Slide the vegetables from the skewers into a large salad bowl. Toss the vegetables with the pesto; if you prefer a looser consistency, add more oil. Serve warm with bread and pasta.

Yield: 4 servings

Grilled Vegetables with Hummus

—■—

MIDDLE EAST

Hummus is an enticing condiment for grilled vegetables. The combination of crushed chick-peas and sesame seed paste gives grilled vegetables a nutty and toasty flavor. For an herbal twist, add fresh mint, marjoram, or sage to it. It also goes well with grilled trout or baby salmon.

For the hummus:
2 cups cooked or canned chick-peas
1/4 cup lemon juice
1/4 cup tahini (sesame paste)
1/4 cup water
2 garlic cloves, minced
1/4 teaspoon salt
1/4 teaspoon ground white pepper

1 medium onion, quartered
2 green or red bell peppers, seeded and halved
1 medium unpeeled eggplant, chopped
1 summer squash, chopped
12 to 16 mushrooms

Combine all of the hummus ingredients in a food processor fitted with a steel blade and process for 15 to 20 seconds, or until the mixture has the consistency of pancake batter. Stop and scrape the sides at least once during the process. Transfer to a serving bowl and chill until ready to serve.

Preheat the grill until the coals are gray to white.

When the fire is ready, thread the vegetables onto skewers and place on the oiled grill. Baste with a little oil if you'd like. Grill for 7 to 10 minutes, turning after about 5 minutes. As the vegetables soften and develop grid marks, pull them off the grill.

Transfer the vegetables to serving plates and serve with the hummus. Rice or pasta makes a good accompaniment.

Yield: 4 servings

Roasted Plantains with Ground Nut Sauce

AFRICA

Ground nuts and goober nuts are African names for peanuts. Ground nuts are appreciated much more in African kitchens than in the United States, and inspire a variety of soups, stews and sauces. Sweet, ripe plantains burst with flavor when they are grilled in their skin. Ground nut sauce with roasted or boiled plantains is a popular African dish.

For the sauce:
1 tablespoon vegetable oil
1 small onion, finely chopped
1 chili pepper, seeded and minced
1 tablespoon minced fresh ginger
1 cup crunchy peanut butter
3/4 cup water
2 tablespoons tomato puree
1 teaspoon ground thyme
1/2 teaspoon salt

4 yellow plantains, ends removed and unpeeled

To make the sauce, heat the oil in a saucepan and add the onion, chili and ginger. Sauté for 5 to 7 minutes. Blend in the peanut butter, water, tomato puree and seasonings. Cook over low heat for 5 to 10 minutes, stirring frequently. Transfer to a serving bowl and keep warm.

Preheat the grill until the coals are gray to white.

When the fire is ready, place the plantains on the grill. Grill for 7 to 10 minutes, turning after about 5 minutes, until the skin is charred and the flesh is soft and yellow.

Transfer to a cutting board and split the skin lengthwise down the middle with a knife. Peel away the skin and cut each plantain into 4 sections. Place the plantains on serving plates and serve with the ground nut sauce over the top.

Yield: 4 servings

Bourbon-Spiked Campfire Beans

— ∎ —

USA

What would a campfire be without baked beans? Here's a healthful version, flavored with a hint of bourbon. For best results, soak the beans overnight and drain and discard the soaking liquid.

1 cup dried navy or Great Northern beans, soaked overnight
4 cups water
2 tablespoons vegetable oil
1 medium size onion, diced
2 garlic cloves, minced
1/2 cup catsup
1/2 cup bourbon
1/3 cup molasses
1/3 cup brown sugar
2 tablespoons Worcestershire sauce
1/2 teaspoon ground allspice
1/4 teaspoon ground black pepper
1/4 teaspoon salt

Place the beans and water in a saucepan and cook over medium heat for about 1 hour, until tender. Drain the beans and discard the liquid.

In a flameproof casserole or Dutch oven, heat the oil and add the onion and garlic. Sauté for about 5 minutes. Stir in the catsup, bourbon, molasses, brown sugar, and Worcestershire sauce and seasonings and cook for 3 to 4 minutes more. Add the beans and mix well.

Preheat the grill until the coals are gray to white.

When the fire is ready, cover the casserole dish and place on the grill over low heat. Cook for 45 minutes to 1 hour, stirring occasionally.

When the beans are thick and steaming with flavor, remove from the heat. Serve with any grilled dish.

Yield: 4 servings

Grilled Vegetables with Sun-Dried Tomato Vinaigrette

USA/ITALY

A vinaigrette is a marriage of oil and vinegar. Out of this union have come myriad variations. The sun-dried tomato vinaigrette is one of the most robust and flavorful. It deliciously heightens the grilled vegetables with a deep tomato flavor.

1/2 cup sun-dried tomatoes
1/3 cup red wine vinegar
3 to 4 garlic cloves, chopped
2 tablespoons chopped fresh basil leaves
1/2 cup plus 2 tablespoons olive oil
1/2 teaspoon ground black pepper
1/2 teaspoon salt
8 to 10 mushrooms
2 cups cubed eggplant
2 medium onions, quartered
1 yellow zucchini or summer squash, chopped
2 bell peppers, seeded and coarsely chopped
1/2 pound mozzarella or provolone cheese, cubed

Soak the dried tomatoes in water for 30 minutes. Drain the liquid and chop the tomatoes.

Add the tomatoes, vinegar, garlic, and basil to a food processor fitted with a steel blade. Process for 15 seconds, until smooth. Add the oil and seasonings and process for 10 seconds more. Transfer to a large bowl.

Preheat the grill until the coals are gray to white.

Thread the vegetables onto skewers. When the fire is ready, place the vegetables on the grill. Grill for 7 to 10 minutes, until tender. Slide the vegetables from the skewers into a large salad bowl.

Combine with the cheese and sun-dried tomato vinaigrette and mix well. Serve warm with bread.

Yield: 4 servings

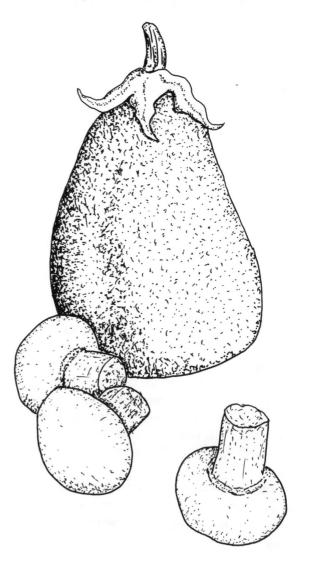

Index
